Reading Comprehension

Grade 6

Copyright © 2014 by Houghton Mifflin Harcourt Publishing Company

All rights reserved. No part of this work may be reproduced or transmitted in any form or by any means, electronic or mechanical, including photocopying or recording, or by any information storage or retrieval system, without the prior written permission of the copyright owner unless such copying is expressly permitted by federal copyright law.

Permission is hereby granted to individuals to photocopy entire pages from this publication in classroom quantities for instructional use and not for resale. Requests for information on other matters regarding duplication of this work should be addressed to Houghton Mifflin Harcourt Publishing Company, Attn: Contracts, Copyrights, and Licensing, 9400 Southpark Center Loop, Orlando, Florida 32819-8647.

Common Core State Standards © Copyright 2010. National Governors Association Center for Best Practices and Council of Chief State School Officers. All rights reserved.

This product is not sponsored or endorsed by the Common Core State Standards Initiative of the National Governors Association Center for Best Practices and the Council of Chief State School Officers.

Printed in the U.S.A.

ISBN 978-0-544-26770-1

1 2 3 4 5 6 7 8 9 10 0982 22 21 20 19 18 17 16 15 14

4500460777 A B C D E F G

If you have received these materials as examination copies free of charge, Houghton Mifflin Harcourt Publishing Company retains title to the materials and they may not be resold. Resale of examination copies is strictly prohibited.

Possession of this publication in print format does not entitle users to convert this publication, or any portion of it, into electronic format.

Dear Parent,

Welcome to the *Core Skills Reading Comprehension* series! You have selected a unique book that focuses on developing your child's comprehension skills, the reading and thinking processes associated with the printed word. Because this series was designed by experienced reading professionals, your child will have reading success as well as gain a firm understanding of the necessary skills outlined in the Common Core State Standards.

Reading should be a fun, relaxed activity for children. They should read selections that relate to or build on their own experiences. Vocabulary should be presented in a sequential and logical progression. The selections in this series build on these philosophies to insure your child's reading success. Other important features in this series that will further aid your child include:

- Short reading selections of interest to a young reader.

- Vocabulary introduced in context and repeated often.

- Comprehension skills applied in context to make the reading more relevant.

- Multiple-choice exercises that develop skills for standardized test taking.

You may wish to have your child read the selections silently or orally, but you will find that sharing the selections and activities with your child will provide additional confidence and support to succeed. When learners experience success, learning becomes a continuous process moving them onward to higher achievements. Moreover, the more your child reads, the more proficient she or he will become.

Enjoy this special time with your child!

Sincerely,
The Educators and Staff of Houghton Mifflin Harcourt

© Houghton Mifflin Harcourt Publishing Company

Core Skills Reading Comprehension
GRADE 6

Table of Contents

© Houghton Mifflin Harcourt Publishing Company

Skills Correlation

LANGUAGE ARTS SKILL	SELECTION
LITERATURE SKILLS	
*Analyzing Word Choice	1, 2, 4, 13
Cause and Effect	2, 9, 10, 12
*Characters	1, 2, 4, 11, 12
*Comparing and Contrasting Texts in Different Genres	2
Details	1, 2, 4, 9
Dialect	1
Literary Genres	1, 12
*Main Idea	8, 10, 11
*Making Inferences	1, 2, 4, 10, 11, 12
Mood	13
*Point of View and Narrator/Speaker	2, 4, 11
Prediction	2, 10
Sequence of Events	2, 9, 12
*Setting	1, 9, 12
*Structure/Plot of a Literary Work	1, 2, 4, 8, 10, 11
*Summarizing Text	4, 9, 11
Theme	10
Tone	2, Skills Review: Selections 1–7, 9, 10, 11
*Using Text Evidence	1, 2, 9
INFORMATIONAL TEXT SKILLS	
*Author's Point of View	6, 7
*Author's Purpose	2, 3, 7
Cause and Effect	6, 7
*Comparing and Contrasting Accounts of Same Event	6, 7
Details	6, 7, 10, 13, Skills Review: Selections 8–13
*Integrating Information/Text Features	3, 6, 13
*Introduction and Elaboration of Individuals, Events, or Ideas	3, 6, 13
*Main Idea	6, 7, 9, 10, Skills Review: Selections 8–13
*Making Inferences	3, 6, 8, 13
Sequence	3, 6, 13
*Structure of Informational Text/Organization	3, 6, 7, 13
*Summarizing Text	7, 13
Tone	6, 7, Skills Review: Selections 1–7
Topic Sentences	9, 10, Skills Review: Selections 8–13
*Using Text Evidence (including to Support Claims)	3, 6, 7, 13

*Aligns to the Common Core State Standards for English Language Arts for grade 6

© Houghton Mifflin Harcourt Publishing Company

Skills Correlation, continued

LANGUAGE ARTS SKILL	SELECTION
VOCABULARY AND DECODING	
Analogies	4, Skills Review: Selections 1–7
Antonyms	12, Skills Review: Selections 8–13
*Figurative Language	2, 7, Skills Review: Selections 1–7, 8, 10
*Idioms	2, Skills Review: Selections 1–7
Multiple-Meaning Words	4, 10, Skills Review: Selections 1–7
Synonyms	10, Skills Review: Selections 8–13
*Technical Words	3
Word Meaning	3, 5, 7, 8, 11, 13
*Words in Context	1, 3, 4, 6, 7, 9, 12
RESEARCH AND STUDY SKILLS	
Determining Fact Versus Fiction	13, Skills Review: Selections 8–13
Evaluating Sources of Information	5, 13, Skills Review: Selections 8–13
Graphic Sources	3, 8
Outlining	3, Skills Review: Selections 1–7
Persuasive Methods/Propaganda	13, Skills Review: Selections 8–13
Skimming	8, 11
Using an Encyclopedia	5
Using an Index	5, Skills Review: Selections 1–7

*Aligns to the Common Core State Standards for English Language Arts for grade 6

© Houghton Mifflin Harcourt Publishing Company

Selection 1: Paired

John Henry was an African American who worked with a crew laying down railroad tracks in the 1800s. He was a "steel driver," a worker who hammered small pieces of steel called spikes into the ground. At one point, his crew had to blast through a mountain before they could lay down the tracks. John Henry's job was to hammer spikes into solid rock. Then the holes made by the spikes would be filled by another worker with dynamite. The explosions gradually created a tunnel through the mountain.

A story was told about John Henry in which a white man challenged him: Could he hammer the steel spikes along a greater distance through the mountain than a steam-powered drilling machine could? Here is a poem based on that story. No one knows who wrote the poem. But it has different versions and, over the years, it has been turned into many songs.

John Henry

by Anonymous

John Henry was about three days old,
Sitting on his papa's knee.
He picked up a hammer and a little piece of steel
Said: "Hammer's gonna be the death of me, Lord, Lord!
Hammer's gonna be the death of me."

The captain says to John Henry,
"Gonna bring me a steam drill 'round,
Gonna bring that steam drill out on the job,
Gonna whop that steel on down, Lord, Lord!
Whop that steel on down."

3   John Henry told his captain,
"A man ain't nothin' but a man
But before I let your steam drill beat me down
I'd die with a hammer in my hand, Lord, Lord!
I'd die with a hammer in my hand."

4   John Henry said to his shaker1,
"Shaker, why don't you sing?
I'm throwin' thirty pounds from my hips on down.
Just listen to that cold steel ring, Lord, Lord!
Listen to that cold steel ring."

¹ **shaker:** the worker who holds the steel spike while it is hammered

1

5   John Henry said to his shaker,
"Shaker, you'd better pray,
'Cause if I miss that little piece of steel,
Tomorrow be your buryin' day, Lord, Lord!
Tomorrow be your buryin' day."

The shaker said to John Henry,
"I think this mountain's cavin' in!"
John Henry said to his shaker, "Man,
That ain't nothin' but my hammer suckin' wind, Lord, Lord!
Nothin' but my hammer suckin' wind."

The man that invented the steam drill,
Thought he was mighty fine.
But John Henry drove his fifteen feet,
And the steam drill only made nine, Lord, Lord!
The steam drill only made nine.

John Henry hammered in the mountain,
His hammer was striking fire,
But he worked so hard, he broke his poor heart,
He laid down his hammer and he died, Lord, Lord!
He laid down his hammer and he died.

They took John Henry to the graveyard,
And they buried him in the sand,
And every locomotive comes a-roaring by,
Says, "There lies a steel-driving man, Lord, Lord!
There lies a steel-driving man."

Well, every Monday morning
When the bluebirds begin to sing
You can hear John Henry a mile or more
You can hear John Henry's hammer ring, Lord, Lord!
You can hear John Henry's hammer ring.

© Houghton Mifflin Harcourt Publishing Company

Name _____ Date _____

Ⓐ Circle the correct answer for each question.

1. How does the location of the contest in the mountains help set the mood for the poem?
   a. It creates a feeling of calmness.
   b. It creates a feeling of nervous energy.
   c. It creates a feeling of hope.
   d. It creates a feeling of coming adventure.

2. To which sense do the last two lines in the fourth stanza appeal?
   a. sight
   b. smell
   c. hearing
   d. touch

3. In the fifth stanza, John Henry tells the shaker that "if I miss that little piece of steel / Tomorrow be your buryin' day." What does John Henry mean?
   a. If John Henry does not hit the steel spike correctly, the blow will kill the shaker.
   b. If John Henry hits the shaker instead of the steel spike, it will kill the shaker.
   c. If John Henry does not beat the steam-powered drill, he will kill the shaker.
   d. If John Henry misses the steel spike, he will get angry and hit the shaker.

4. Based on the context of the eighth stanza, what does the word *fire* mean?
   a. dynamite
   b. flame
   c. red rocks
   d. sparks

5. What is the effect of the repetition in the last two lines of each stanza?
   a. It creates a regular rhyme.
   b. It makes John Henry seem like a real person.
   c. It echoes the sound of John Henry's hammer.
   d. It allows the speaker to express John Henry's true feelings.

6. Who or what keeps John Henry's name alive for all time?
   a. the locomotives
   b. the mountain
   c. the bluebirds
   d. the other workers

3

© Houghton Mifflin Harcourt Publishing Company

7. Which line **best** shows how determined John Henry is to beat the steam-powered drill?

a. *"A man ain't nothin' but a man"*

b. *"Just listen to that cold steel ring."*

c. John Henry hammered in the mountain,

d. His hammer was striking fire,

B **Answer the questions on the lines provided.**

1. Why do you think the poet uses the word *whop* in the second stanza?

I Think The word whop means John henry hammered in The mountain

2. Describe John Henry's attitude at the start of the contest with the steam-powered drill. Use support from the poem in your answer.

John Henry's attitude at The start of The story. he was

upset

3. Use two examples from the poem to describe how the contest between John Henry and the steam-powered drill ended.

his Broke his The he Broke his heart

he laid down his hammer and he died

C **Dialect is the way a particular group of people speaks. The way they speak may be influenced by factors such as where they live, the time in which they live, or their background. Everyone speaks some kind of dialect. The dialect that is the most common in a country usually becomes accepted as the standard way of speaking.**

> **DIALECT:**   Jody ain't fixin' to move, is she?
>
> **STANDARD:** Jody isn't about to move, is she?

Read "John Henry" again to see when dialect is used and when standard speech is used. Then on the lines provided, write your analysis of the use of dialect in the poem. Be sure to describe the effect that the use of dialect has on the reader.

The standrd speech is used

and dialect.

© Houghton Mifflin Harcourt Publishing Company

Read the characteristics of a legend.

Characteristics of a Legend

- A legend can be in the form of a story, poem, or song.
- It is usually based on at least some historical fact or includes some element of truth.
- It has been handed down from generation to generation.
- It has often come into being around a well-known or heroic figure or a famous event.
- In many cases, it has an important meaning for the culture in which it was first told.

D Could "John Henry" be considered a legend? Think about the introduction to "John Henry" and about the poem itself. Then answer the questions on the lines provided. Except for question 5, be sure to provide support for your answers.

1. On what, if any, historical fact do you think "John Henry" is based?

   _____

   _____

2. Do you think that "John Henry" has been handed down from generation to generation?

   _____

   _____

   _____

3. Do you think that "John Henry" came into being around a well-known or heroic figure or a famous event?

   _____

   _____

   _____

4. Do you think that "John Henry" had an important meaning for the culture in which it was first told?

   _____

   _____

   _____

5. Do you think that "John Henry" is a legend? _____

5

Selection 2: Paired

Pecos Bill

Pecos Bill was the most famous and spectacular cowboy of the Southwest. Other cowboys sat around their evening campfires during cattle drives, telling stories about Pecos Bill and his fantastic adventures. Some of them were so fantastic that they were a little hard to believe.

They say that when Bill was a year old—and only knee-high to a grasshopper—he left his home in East Texas. His family moved west because another family settled in only fifty miles away and his father thought the place was getting too crowded.

One afternoon, as the family's wagon was crossing the Pecos River, Bill fell out. Since there were sixteen or seventeen other children in the family, it was about a month before anyone noticed he was missing.

Although Bill was lost, not for one minute did he ever feel lonely. He grew up living with the coyotes along the Pecos River. In no time at all he had learned their language, how to hunt with them, and how to howl at the moon at night. Not knowing any better, he came to think he was a coyote.

Then one day, when Bill was about ten years old, a cowboy rode by and spotted him. Bill had just been in a fight with a couple of grizzly bears and had hugged them to death. The cowboy asked Bill, "Why are you living like a varmint¹?"

Bill replied, "I ain't a varmint. I'm a coyote."

The cowboy said, "Son, you're a human boy."

"I don't believe you," said Bill. "Look at my fleas. And I live with coyotes and howl all night just like they do."

"That doesn't prove anything," the cowboy responded. "Lots of Texans have fleas, and plenty of them howl. Coyotes all have tails, though, and you don't. Therefore, you can't be a coyote."

Bill had to admit that he didn't have a tail. Then he had to admit that he wasn't a coyote after all.

Reluctantly accepting that he was human, Bill moved into town to live with others of his kind. There, he got mixed up with a bunch of wild fellows and became a cowboy—but not any ordinary cowboy. The older he got, the bigger, stronger, and tougher he got, too. Everyone started calling him Pecos Bill.

It took a while, but Pecos Bill finally got over missing his coyote family. Human company was even becoming downright tolerable at times. But there was one thing he just couldn't abide. That was all the talking. Yak, yak, yak. So he didn't usually pay much attention to the conversations in his vicinity.

¹ **varmint:** an animal that is considered a pest

One day, though, Bill heard something that caused his head to whip around. "That white stallion was breathing fire," one of the cowboys was saying. "He galloped by so fast, a cyclone stopped in its tracks to watch him pass by. His tail and mane were like bolts of lightning. Whatever made us think we could catch that horse?"

"Durned if I know," piped up another cowboy. "Six of us in hot pursuit, all day and all night for a whole week. And that stallion ran every last one of our best horses right into the ground. In fact, Lightning never even broke into a sweat."

"Uh, pardon me for overhearing," interrupted Pecos Bill, "but do you all happen to know where I might find this Lightning? Sounds like he and I would get along just fine."

The cowboys directed Pecos Bill to the Powder River. Sure enough, before long he saw the white stallion gallop by, his hooves barely touching the ground. Pecos knew at once that the astounding creature would be his. He jumped off his horse and took off after the stallion, running like the wind.

Lightning got a good laugh out of a man trying to catch him on foot. But while he was laughing, Pecos Bill came right up on his heels. For four days and nights the man stuck with the horse, from Mexico to Canada and back, and twice around the state of Texas.

Although he wasn't even breathing heavily, Lightning was getting tired of this game. So he neighed and brayed and tried to grind Pecos Bill under his hooves. But before the first hoof could touch the ground, Pecos had turned a twisting somersault and landed right on Lightning's back.

Now Lightning had certainly never had a man on his back before, and he didn't like it one bit. So he tried to shake the man off going at top speed. In less than twenty seconds, he had covered two miles.

But Pecos Bill refused to fall off. Lightning bucked—sideways, wideways, and every whichways. But Pecos Bill still held on.

Then Lightning scraped Pecos Bill up against every tree and rock in the state. Bill was ragged and bleeding, but he hadn't budged an inch.

Finally, as Lightning reared up and over on his back, Bill leaped off and pinned the horse under his foot. The stallion struggled for a while, but Pecos Bill stroked his neck and talked to him in the language of the animals. He said they were both wild spirits and would have many wonderful adventures together.

And that's exactly what happened.

7

© Houghton Mifflin Harcourt Publishing Company

Name _____ Date _____

Ⓐ Circle the correct answer for each question.

1. Why did Bill's father move his family away from East Texas?

   a. He wanted his family to see what West Texas was like.

   b. He wanted his sons to grow up to be cowboys.

   c. He wanted to live in an area where coyotes roamed.

   d. He wanted to live in an area with fewer people.

2. What was Pecos Bill's opinion of the other cowboys?

   a. He thought they could be lazy at times.

   b. He thought they talked too much.

   c. He thought they were not very tough.

   d. He thought they rarely told the truth.

3. Read this sentence from the selection.

   > "In fact, Lightning never even broke into a sweat."

   The author included this line of dialogue to show that Lightning

   a. was able to outrun the other horses without much effort.

   b. was constantly surrounded by intense heat.

   c. was able to generate heat to make him run faster.

   d. was more intelligent than the cowboys who chased him.

4. Why did Lightning scrape Pecos Bill against trees and rocks?

   a. Lightning wanted Pecos Bill to either die or get seriously injured.

   b. Lightning was uncomfortable with the feeling of a rider on his back.

   c. Lightning remembered Pecos Bill from a previous encounter.

   d. Lightning wanted to prove his strength to Pecos Bill.

5. If Pecos Bill had *not* leaped off Lightning when he did, then Pecos Bill probably

   a. would have been carried off by Lightning and gotten lost for a long time.

   b. would have been carried off by Lightning to live with wild stallions.

   c. would have been rescued from Lightning by his own horse.

   d. would have been pinned to the ground by Lightning.

© Houghton Mifflin Harcourt Publishing Company

6. Which two words *best* describe Pecos Bill?

   a. stubborn and silly

   b. strong and determined

   c. solitary but content

   d. confused but adventurous

7. Based on information in the selection, the reader can conclude that Pecos Bill

   a. kept Lightning for the rest of his life.

   b. spent most of his life in West Texas.

   c. related more easily to animals than to people.

   d. rarely trusted what cowboys told him.

8. Which of these happened first in the selection?

   a. Bill searched for a horse.

   b. Bill moved to a town.

   c. Bill overheard some cowboys talking.

   d. Bill stopped missing the coyotes he had lived with.

B Answer the questions on the lines provided.

1. Pecos Bill told Lightning that they were both "wild spirits." Name at least two details from the selection that are evidence that Bill was a wild spirit.

   _____

   _____

   _____

2. What do you think is the author's point of view toward Pecos Bill? Give reasons for your answer.

   _____

   _____

   _____

9

An idiom is a word or phrase that means something that is different from the literal meaning of each word. For example, if someone tells you he is **on top of the world**, he isn't actually on top of the world, since that would be impossible. He means that he is feeling very happy about something.

Read this sentence from the selection about Pecos Bill: **Bill was ragged and bleeding, but he hadn't budged an inch.** Bill didn't pull out a ruler and measure how much he had or hadn't moved. **Not to budge an inch** means not to move at all.

C **Read the following items. If the item contains an idiom, underline the idiom and then write the letter of the meaning of the idiom on the line before the number. For the one item that doesn't contain an idiom, write an X on the line before the number. Use a dictionary if you need help.**

_____ 1. Pecos Bill was knee-high to a grasshopper when his family moved away from West Texas.

_____ 2. "You're pulling my leg," Pecos Bill said when the cowboy told him about Lightning. Yet the cowboy insisted that the stallion really did exist.

_____ 3. For a whole week, the cowboys were in hot pursuit of the stallion.

_____ 4. Lightning's tail and mane were like bolts of lightning.

_____ 5. "Keep your chin up," Pecos Bill told the cowboy after he had been thrown from a wild horse for the tenth time. "Soon enough you'll have that horse tamed."

_____ 6. It was only once in a blue moon that Pecos Bill took a bath. Everyone wished he would bathe more often.

_____ 7. Pecos Bill found some of the townspeople to be tight-fisted. He believed everyone should be generous with their money.

_____ 8. Pecos Bill thought living with coyotes had been a piece of cake. But nobody he talked to could imagine having done something that difficult.

a. teasing me

b. very young and small

c. very easy

d. stingy

e. rarely

f. be brave in spite of problems

g. trying hard to get or catch something

10

Name _____ Date _____

D **Think about the poem "John Henry" and the selection "Pecos Bill." Then answer the questions on the lines provided.**

1. What did John Henry and Pecos Bill have in common?

   _____

   _____

   _____

2. Would you consider both John Henry and Pecos Bill successful? Explain your answer.

   _____

   _____

3. Different kinds of conflicts can occur in selections and poems.

   • a person against another person

   • a person against something in nature

   • a person against himself or herself

   • a person against society or something produced by society

   Is the kind of conflict that occurred in "John Henry" and in "Pecos Bill" the same or different? Explain your answer.

   _____

   _____

   _____

4. The *tone* of a text is the attitude the writer has toward a character, toward the audience, or toward the subject of the work. The writer's choice of words and details give clues about the tone. Below are some examples of words that describe tone.

playful	objective	humorous	sympathetic
serious	passionate	admiring	positive
sarcastic	disapproving	respectful	sorrowful

   Write two words from the list that describe the tone of "John Henry" and two words that describe the tone of "Pecos Bill."

   _____

   _____

11

© Houghton Mifflin Harcourt Publishing Company

E **Hyperbole is a figure of speech that uses an incredible exaggeration. An exaggeration is an overstating of an idea.**

1. A writer may use hyperbole to make a character or event seem impressive to readers. Circle the letter of each detail about John Henry that includes hyperbole.

   a. John Henry was about three days old when he said, "Hammer's gonna be the death of me."

   b. John Henry told the captain, "I'd die with a hammer in my hand."

   c. John Henry said, "That ain't nothin' but my hammer suckin' wind."

2. Often a writer uses hyperbole to create humor. Circle the letter of each detail from "Pecos Bill" that includes hyperbole.

   a. Bill's family moved west because another family settled in only fifty miles away and his father thought the place was getting too crowded.

   b. After Bill fell out of the wagon, it was about a month before anyone in Bill's family noticed he was missing.

   c. Then one day a cowboy rode by and spotted Pecos Bill.

   d. Bill had just been in a fight with a couple of grizzly bears and had hugged them to death.

   e. The older Pecos Bill got, the bigger, stronger, and tougher he became.

   f. Lightning galloped by so fast, a cyclone stopped in its tracks to watch him pass by.

   g. For days and nights Pecos Bill stuck with the horse, from Mexico to Canada and back, and twice around the state of Texas.

3. Now it's your turn. Revise these sentences so that they include hyperbole.

   a. The bolt of lightning lit up the front yard.

   _____

   _____

   b. The rain came down harder than I'd ever seen it.

   _____

   _____

   c. The sun was really hot that day.

   _____

   _____

   d. The temperature dropped quickly during the night.

   _____

   _____

© Houghton Mifflin Harcourt Publishing Company

Selection 3

Throughout history, in every part of the world, people have needed or wanted things that they did not make or grow or catch themselves. Long ago, when there was no such thing as money, the only way people could get these things was by trading, or *bartering*. People bartered with one another for food and for goods such as clothes, tools, ornaments, cloth, and furniture.

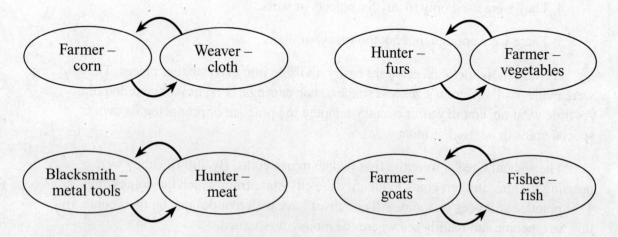

Bartering worked very well as long as people lived simple lives. However, when people began needing and wanting more and more things, life became more complicated. Trading to get just the thing they wanted could take a very long time. Another problem was that the Smiths, Farmers, Hunters, and Fishers could not always agree on how much one large fish, one beautiful bearskin, five pounds of carrots, or fifty colorful shells and beads were worth.

The Farmers also had trouble dragging heavy sacks of onions over to the Smiths' forge to trade for a new metal knife. Mrs. Diggs had to balance a heavy basket on her head to swap the salt she had dug up for the garment Mr. Tailor put together from the cloth he had received from Mrs. Weaver.

Then someone had a brilliant idea. Instead of everyone trading different things, people could agree on one common thing that could be used to pay for other things. There had to be something that almost everyone would accept—something that was special enough that people would take it in payment for their goods or their work.

People tried many different items, yet there were things that not everyone had a use for, such as Mr. Wright's wheels or Mrs. Herd's goats. Finally, they decided on small pieces of metal. The type of metal depended on what was available in a region; however, some of the metals used were copper, bronze, iron, brass, tin, lead, silver, and gold.

© Houghton Mifflin Harcourt Publishing Company

These pieces of metal were the world's first money. The following characteristics made them an easier way to pay for goods and work:

1. They were durable, that is, they would last for a long time.

2. They were portable, or easy to carry.

3. They were convenient to use.

4. They were used only to pay for objects or work.

5. There were enough, but not too many, of them.

At first, these metal pieces were easily divisible into even smaller pieces. They were made in all different sizes and shapes, such as rings, bars, knives, and dolphins. As time went on, country after country adopted the practice of producing its own special coins to be used as money.

The ancient Greeks were the first people to use coins. By 700 BC, they were pressing designs on their coins to identify the city-state from which the coins came. This practice still goes on today. All countries have different designs on their coins. In this way, people can readily see where the money was issued.

Early on, dishonest people would sometimes shave the metal off the edges of the coins, melt down the metal, and produce new coins. One of the last changes made in coins was to put a special edging around each one. This step made it possible for the person receiving the money to tell at once whether someone had tampered with the rim of a coin.

A **Circle the correct answer for each question.**

1. What did people do before they used pieces of metal for payment?
   a. They stamped coins.
   b. They traded one thing for another.
   c. They used paper money.
   d. They produced everything they needed.

2. Look at the diagram after the first paragraph of the selection. What is its purpose?
   a. to show examples of bartering
   b. to show how people long ago led simple lives
   c. to show how bartering could create problems
   d. to show different jobs people had in the time of bartering

© Houghton Mifflin Harcourt Publishing Company

3. Why must coins be durable?

   a. They have to be divided into smaller amounts.

   b. They have to be handled by many people.

   c. They have to last for hundreds of years.

   d. They have to be easy to carry.

4. The third paragraph of the selection makes the **best** evidence for which of these statements in the selection?

   a. *Long ago, when there was no such thing as money, the only way people could get these things was by trading, or* bartering.

   b. *Bartering worked very well as long as people lived simple lives.*

   c. *Trading to get just the thing they wanted could take a very long time.*

   d. *Instead of trading different things, people could agree on one common thing that could be used to pay for other things.*

5. Read these sentences from the eighth paragraph of the selection.

   > All countries have different designs on their coins. In this way, people can readily see where the money was issued.

   Which phrase in the eighth paragraph helps you understand the word *issued*?

   a. *people can readily see*

   c. *from which the coins came*

   b. *practice still goes on*

   d. *first people to use coins*

6. Why did the author most likely write this selection?

   a. to persuade readers to collect coins from the past

   b. to give information on the development of coins

   c. to entertain readers with stories about people from long ago

   d. to explain why he or she thinks using money is better than bartering

B Answer the questions on the lines provided.

1. Why does the author discuss bartering even though the topic of the selection is coins?

   _____

   _____

2. Why can the fourth paragraph be considered a "turning point" in the selection?

   _____

   _____

15

Name _____ Date _____

C Deposit these coins in the bank by writing the correct word next to each meaning.

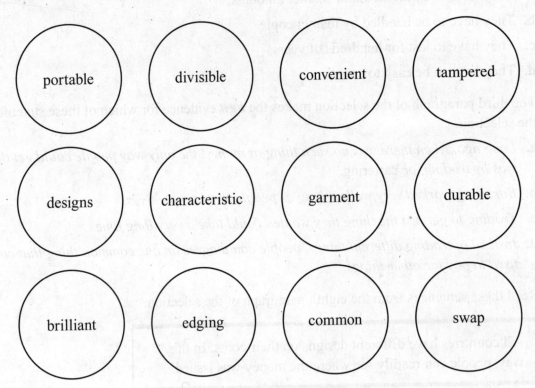

portable	divisible	convenient	tampered
designs	characteristic	garment	durable
brilliant	edging	common	swap

1. can be made into smaller parts _____

2. patterns _____

3. found everywhere _____

4. easy to use, do, or get _____

5. a feature or quality _____

6. a piece of clothing _____

7. very smart _____

8. to trade _____

9. easily carried _____

10. lasts for a long time _____

11. interfered with _____

© Houghton Mifflin Harcourt Publishing Company

Outlines are a way to make information more compact and easier to remember. An outline is also a good way to organize information in your own words. Outlining will keep you from copying word-for-word from reference books.

Here is the form to use to outline information.

Title
(The title explains the topic of the whole article.)

(This is the **main idea** of the first paragraph.) → I.

A.
B. (These are the supporting details of the first paragraph. They are called **subtopics**.)
C.
D.

(This is the main idea of the second paragraph. Main ideas use Roman numerals.) → II.

A.
B. (These are the subtopics of the second paragraph. Subtopics use capital letters.)
C.

1.
2. (This is additional information, or supporting details, for subtopic C. These use Arabic numbers.)
3.

D Before 1776, the thirteen colonies on the east coast of the present-day United States belonged to England, which was called the "mother country." Study this outline. Then answer the questions that follow.

A History of Money in the American Colonies

I. Coins were scarce in the colonies.

   A. England would not send coins to the colonies.

   B. England did not permit the colonies to make their own coins.

      1. England wanted colonists to be loyal and dependent.

      2. England wanted the colonies to trade only with the mother country.

      3. Other countries wanted money for the products they sold to the colonies.

II. Colonists bartered goods instead of using cash.

   A. Beaver pelts were traded.

   B. Grains were traded.

   C. Musket balls and nails were made in the colonies and traded.

   D. The Virginia and Maryland colonies traded in tobacco.

   E. Native American wampum beads made from shells were accepted as money by other colonies and Native Americans.

17

III. Coins from other countries were left in the colonies by sailors whose ships came there.
    A. English shillings
    B. French coins
    C. Dutch coins
    D. Spanish coins called "pieces of eight"
        1. Spanish coins could be chopped into 8 pie-shaped pieces.
        2. These pieces, called "bits," were used for smaller change.

IV. In 1652, the Massachusetts Colony started making coins.
    A. The coins were silver.
        1. Pine tree shillings were worth 3 pennies.
        2. Oak tree shillings were worth 6 pennies.
        3. Designs were stamped on the coins.
    B. Massachusetts was breaking English law by making coins.
    C. Only the English kings could issue coins.
    D. From 1652 until 1776, all Massachusetts coins were dated 1652.
        1. In 1652, England had no king to issue coins.
        2. No law was broken by Massachusetts.

V. Massachusetts was the first colony to produce paper money.
    A. In 1690, it issued notes called *bills of credit*.
    B. These notes financed the first French and Indian War.
        1. This was a war between the French and English colonies.
        2. It was fought for the control of eastern North America.

VI. By 1775, the colonies were ready to rebel against England.
    A. Each colony issued its own paper money to pay for the Revolutionary War.
    B. The Continental Congress issued its own paper money.

© Houghton Mifflin Harcourt Publishing Company

1. How many main ideas are in this outline? _____

2. What is the title of this outline?

   _____

3. What is some additional information found in main idea IV, subtopic D?

   a. Massachusetts printed paper money.

   b. There was no English king in 1652.

   c. England did not send coins to the colonies.

   d. The French and Indian War was fought.

4. How many subtopics are found in main idea I? _____

5. What did you learn from main idea II, subtopic C?

   _____

   _____

6. What is main idea II mostly about?

   a. how Spanish coins were cut

   b. how the colonists got Dutch coins

   c. why England wanted the colonies to be dependent

   d. what the early colonists traded

7. What is the purpose of this outline?

   a. to organize facts about money in the American colonies

   b. to organize facts about English trade with the American colonies

   c. to explain the role of the American colonies in the French and Indian War

   d. to encourage people to collect coins issued by the American colonies

8. How many supporting details are found in main idea V, subtopic B?

   _____

9. What were some of the first coins issued by Massachusetts?

   a. pieces of eight   c. pine tree bills of credit

   b. maple leaf pennies   d. pine tree shillings

10. During which war did all the colonies begin to print paper money?

    a. The War of 1812   c. The Revolutionary War

    b. The Civil War   d. The French and Indian War

© Houghton Mifflin Harcourt Publishing Company

Name _____   Date _____

E In 1792, Congress made new coins and a new currency system for the new country, the United States. However, there were still so many foreign coins being used in these former colonies that in 1793 the government declared foreign coins legal and part of the United States currency system. This circle graph shows the percentage of each foreign coin still in use in 1800. Study the information and answer the questions.

Foreign Coins Being Used in the United States in 1800

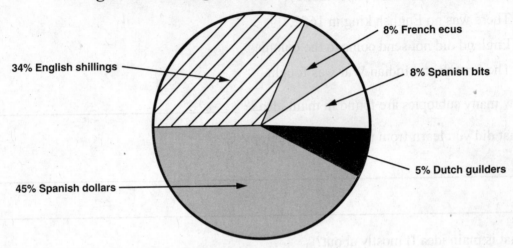

1. Which foreign coins were being used the most?

   _____

2. Which two groups of coins were the same in number?

   _____

3. Of which coins were there the fewest?

   _____

4. What is the difference between the percent of English shillings and the percent of Spanish dollars?

   _____

5. French ecus were what percent of the total of foreign coins? _____

6. Which two groups of coins made up 50% of the total number of foreign coins being used?

   _____

7. What percent of Italian lira were being used?

   a. 40%   **b.** 6%   **c.** The graph does not show this.

8. What does this graph show?

   _____

© Houghton Mifflin Harcourt Publishing Company

Selection 4

Rhymes and Treasure

My name is Belinda Acosta. I've already decided what I want to be when I'm grown: a detective. In fact, for someone my age, I'm already a pretty good detective. My brother Jacob sometimes helps me solve cases. Jacob and I work well together. We both believe that cooperation always gets better results than competition.

My most recent case started with a letter from my grandmother.

Dear Belinda and Jacob,

I have an extremely interesting mystery to solve. I could hardly wait to get started on it myself. But I knew you would enjoy working out this puzzle with me, just as you have in the past. So I've decided not to start my investigation until the day after your school closes for vacation. We'll have a great time solving this case together!

Eagerly,

Grandma Faye

Faye Taylor

P.S. You may bring your mother and father with you.

When we visited Grandma, she told us this story: One of her closest friends, Mrs. McIntosh, had died a few months ago. Because she had no relatives, Mrs. McIntosh left everything in her apartment to our grandmother. The two of them had been very much alike. They loved mysteries and solving puzzles. Mrs. McIntosh's lawyer, a man named Mr. Boaz, told Grandma that there was a treasure hidden among her friend's old books, furniture, china, paintings, clocks, and other antiques. He was supposed to start Grandma off on her search for the treasure.

"She said that hunting for the treasure would keep you from missing her too much," the lawyer told Grandma.

Grandma chuckled and said, "That sounds like Marge McIntosh. What a sense of great humor she had!"

Mr. Boaz said, "I have some clues that Mrs. McIntosh left for you. But I enjoy mysteries, too. If you need help with these, please call me."

© Houghton Mifflin Harcourt Publishing Company

The list the lawyer handed Grandma was titled *Hints*.

HINTS

1. Never throw away anything.
2. The most worthless might in the end become the most wonderful.
3. Happy sleuthing, dear fellow clue chaser.

After Grandma finished telling us the story, she said, "Let's begin our search for the treasure tomorrow." Then she jingled the keys to Mrs. McIntosh's apartment that the lawyer had given her.

The next afternoon Mom, Dad, Jacob, and I picked up Grandma. Then we drove to Mrs. McIntosh's apartment. It was in a huge house that must have been a hundred years old. Jacob and I were amazed at the size of the rooms. But they had to be large because they were stuffed with furniture and antiques of all kinds.

"Where do we start with this weird project?" I asked. "By searching the desk? That's what detectives in mystery books do."

The only trouble was that Mrs. McIntosh had three desks—one in the living room, one in the bedroom, and another in the kitchen.

Mom suggested, "Look at this living room desk with all the pigeonholes. Desks like this often have secret drawers or cabinets."

Jacob darted toward the desk.

We took everything out of the big piece of furniture and looked it over. We tapped the wood, measured, pushed, and pulled. But we didn't find a single clue or secret hiding place!

After we took a break, we turned our attention to the kitchen desk. It had one large drawer, which was empty.

Dad suggested, "Let's look at the back of the desk."

© Houghton Mifflin Harcourt Publishing Company

Name _____ Date _____

It took three of us to pull the heavy desk away from the kitchen wall. As we struggled with it, my knee hit the wooden back. Suddenly a secret door popped open. There I finally discovered our first clue, along with an antique brooch. The piece of jewelry was in the shape of a beetle.

"Marge and I both loved old and unusual jewelry," said Grandma. I heard an unmistakable sadness in her voice.

The clue was on a tiny roll of paper. When Mom spread out the paper, we read a rhyme.

> Hickory, dickory, dock,
> The mouse ran down the clock.
> The clock struck one.
> The mouse was done!
> But you're not through
> Because here's a clue!
> That mouse did not roam.
> It went straight back home!

"The grandfather clock!" exclaimed Grandma. "That's the place to search next."

"We'll start there tomorrow morning. It's late now, and I'm tired," groaned Mom.

The next afternoon, as soon as we unlocked the door to Mrs. McIntosh's apartment, Grandma said, "I've been thinking about that rhyme. It told us that we were reading a clue and that the mouse went home."

"A mouse's home is a hole somewhere," said Jacob.

I remembered something. In cartoons, the mice always pop out of a hole in a baseboard. So Jacob and I crawled all around the rooms, studying the baseboards. We didn't notice anything unusual. But behind one of the beds, we finally found it. A neat little circle was drawn on the white wood. Inside the circle the following words were written: "the resident rodent."

First we shoved the bed aside. Then we removed the baseboard. Behind it was an opening. In the opening Dad discovered a small leather bag containing four gold coins and another slip of paper.

"These are from Marge's coin collection," said Grandma with a sigh. "We both loved collecting old coins."

© Houghton Mifflin Harcourt Publishing Company
Selection 4
Core Skills Reading Comprehension, Grade 6

"There's another rhyme on the paper!" I exclaimed. I read it aloud.

> So you got this far
> And won another clue.
> It shows thinking on your part.
> Good for all of you!
> Now keep on going
> Until you reach the gate.
> Swing it back, swing it forth,
> Before it is too late.

We searched all over the apartment, but no one could see anything that resembled a gate.

"Wait a minute," said Grandma. "Marge would sometimes misspell words by leaving out letters. Maybe she meant grate."

All eyes turned to the fireplace. Jacob and I dug around in the ashes. Mom climbed on Dad's back and up into the chimney. An hour later, my filthy, ash-covered family still hadn't discovered the hiding place for the treasure.

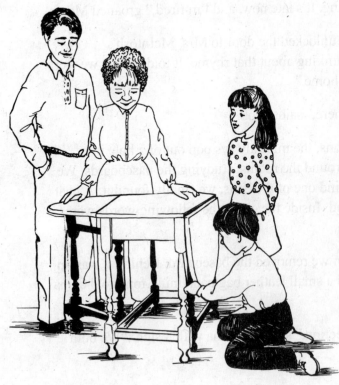

I lay exhausted on the floor staring around the room. "I've got it!" I shouted. "There's a gateleg table in here." I pointed to a thin table that stood against the wall.

After Mom and Grandma had pulled the table into the center of the room, Jacob and I took turns swinging the gatelegs to and fro. Gateleg tables have extra folding legs that can be pulled out. Then the top of the table unfolds and rests on these legs. It changes a small table into one much larger. Yet all that swinging of table legs did nothing to help our investigation.

© Houghton Mifflin Harcourt Publishing Company

"Turn the table upside down," ordered Grandma. "Then move the gatelegs."

What a smart detective Grandma was! There was a small space behind each leg. From one space Grandma pulled out a folded piece of paper. In another space was a plastic bag with a pair of earrings made of solid gold! Everyone had to examine the earrings. It was quite awhile before anyone looked at the note.

Dad was the first to notice. He said, "Hey! There's something hard wrapped in this paper!"

Grandma had the honor of unfolding the note. Inside was a strip of metal that looked like this:

"What is it?" we all asked.

Grandma read the note.

> It's in the room
> Not far from you.
> Look all around
> For an *obvious* clue.
> Use what you found —
> The thing's a key
> To open a lock
> Of something you see.

Everywhere we looked there were locks and keyholes—on drawers, on desks, on doors, on chests, and on boxes. It was too late in the day to start trying to open them with that strange-looking key. We decided to go home and start fresh the next day.

(to be continued)

25

© Houghton Mifflin Harcourt Publishing Company

A **Circle the correct answer for each question.**

1. Why did Mrs. McIntosh arrange the search for clues?
    a. to give Belinda and Jacob a chance to be detectives
    b. to keep Grandma from missing her
    c. to puzzle Mr. Boaz, the lawyer
    d. to give Grandma practice being a detective

2. Read the paragraph that follows the note from Grandma to Belinda and Jacob. Why is this paragraph important to the selection?
    a. It provides the reader an idea of the setting.
    b. It provides details about an important character.
    c. It provides several details about the problem that will be solved.
    d. It provides a hint about Grandma's relationship with Belinda and Jacob.

3. Read this sentence from the selection.

    > Jacob darted toward the desk.

    By using the word *darted*, the author shows that Jacob
    a. did not believe what Mom had said.
    b. wanted to solve the mystery quickly so he could go home.
    c. was eager to solve the mystery and find the treasure.
    d. did not want Belinda to find the treasure first.

4. How did the circle get on the baseboard?
    a. The circle was part of the wood.
    b. A animal made the circle with its teeth.
    c. Grandma planned the circle.
    d. Mrs. McIntosh drew the circle.

5. Which of these is a rodent?
    a. a cat   b. a pigeon   c. a mouse   d. a beetle

6. Which of these do all gateleg tables have?
    a. more than four legs   c. fewer than four legs
    b. a hidden gate   d. extra drawers

7. Based on the selection, which of these *best* describes the person Mrs. McIntosh had been?
    a. She was curious and mysterious.   c. She liked to play mean jokes on people.
    b. She was thoughtful and fun-loving.   d. She wanted to be in charge of things.

© Houghton Mifflin Harcourt Publishing Company

8. Belinda is the narrator of the selection. What does the reader learn about Grandma through Belinda?

   a. Grandma liked to be in command when she solved a mystery with Belinda and Jacob.

   b. Grandma was still a little sad about the death of her friend Mrs. McIntosh.

   c. Grandma wanted to solve a mystery with Mr. Boaz, the lawyer.

   d. Grandma needed help when heavy objects had to be moved.

B **Answer the questions on the lines provided.**

1. Why are Mrs. McIntosh's rhyming notes an important part of the selection?

   _____

   _____

2. Write a brief summary of this part of "Rhymes and Treasure."

   _____

   _____

   _____

   _____

C **Some words have more than one meaning and pronunciation. Study the word below and its meanings. Then write the letter of the correct meaning of the word next to each sentence.**

   project: a. (prō jĕct´) *v*: to throw or cast forward

   b. (prō jĕct´) *v*: to stick out or over something else

   c. (prŏj´ ĕct) *n*: a plan, job, or task

   _____ 1. The roof *projects* over the windows on the top floors.

   _____ 2. Work had just begun on the *project* when it was suddenly interrupted.

   _____ 3. The machine *projects* an image on the screen.

   _____ 4. The shadow of the eagle, *projected* on the snow, alerted the lambs.

   _____ 5. The shoes *projecting* from under the bench were covered with paint.

   _____ 6. Improving his work in fractions and decimals is Jacob's latest *project*.

27

D There are different ways you can compare one thing to another. One way is to compare pairs of things to each other. When doing this, think about how the first two things—that is, the things in the first pair of words—are related to each other. Then apply how these things are related to the two things in the second pair of words. Complete each sentence by circling the correct word.

Examples:

a. A *big circle* is to a *little circle* as a *big square* is to a <u>*little square*</u>.

b. A *shoe* is to a *foot* as a *glove* is to a <u>*hand*</u>. (You wear a shoe on your foot. You wear a glove on your hand.)

c. *Hot* is to *warm* as *cold* is to _____. (The words *hot*, *warm*, and *cold* all deal with temperatures. Which word that expresses temperature would fit in the comparison and make sense?)

   stove   (cool)   snow

1. *Medicine* is to *cure* as *poison* is to _____.

   snakes   kill   drink

2. *Hot* is to *cold* as *safe* is to _____.

   harmless   safety patrol   dangerous

3. *Roar* is to *lion* as *hiss* is to _____.

   boy   snake   elephant

4. *Bee* is to *hive* as *bird* is to _____.

   nest   sing   wings

5. *January* is to *winter* as *July* is to _____.

   spring   summer   fireworks

6. *Hunter* is to *jungle* as *fisher* is to _____.

   boat   water   line

7. *Time* is to *clock* as *temperature* is to _____.

   winter   swimming   thermometer

8. *Venom* is to *snake* as *sting* is to _____.

   bee   pain   butterfly

9. *Artist* is to *paint* as *chef* is to _____.

   oven   engine   stone

© Houghton Mifflin Harcourt Publishing Company

The next day, we could hardly wait to begin our treasure hunt again.

Finding what the key opened was a tiresome job. The strange object fit none of the keyholes and locks in the furniture.

At last, Mom sat down wearily. "This is ridiculous. If we need information, instead of guessing we should go to an expert."

I said, "The library can help us."

"Better yet, before going to the library, let's go to an antique store," suggested Grandma. "Then we'll have something to guide us in our search at the library."

An hour later, we were entering the second antique store. In the first store, no one there had been able to identify the odd key.

The owner of this shop smiled as she heard our question. "I can't tell what the key fits, but I do know it's originally from some part of Asia. There's a store down the street that sells Asian antiques, such as oriental rugs."

The owner of the next shop nodded his head as he looked at our key. "It unlocks a certain kind of Korean wooden box with heavy brass decorations. The lock is usually shaped like an animal and is very fancy. Somewhere on the lock will be a hole into which you push the key. It causes the whole lock to come apart."

© Houghton Mifflin Harcourt Publishing Company

Unfortunately, the owner had no boxes with locks of that sort to show us. So off we trekked to the library. Two hours later, we returned to the apartment with a few books on Korean boxes.

"I haven't seen anything around here that looks like any of these," I complained.

We looked high and low, in and out. This time our eagle-eyed mom spotted it. She was examining a corner table with a marble top. The three wooden legs were spread apart on the floor, but they got closer together as they neared the tabletop. Sneaky Mrs. McIntosh had slipped the Korean box into a space where the legs were close enough together to hold it. When seen from a distance, the box seemed to be a part of the table.

Now, was our suspense over? Would we finally see the treasure? Inside the box was an embroidered silk scarf. We unfolded the lovely fabric and found tiny figures of ivory and jade. One was an ivory figure of an ancient Japanese soldier with a sword. Another was a jade statue of a plump man. There also was a Japanese fish of purple jade with curly fins and a huge grin on its face. Jacob's favorite was a tiny ivory octopus with eight curling tentacles and a puzzled expression. The one that made me shiver was a hideous ivory rat with a long tail.

"We haven't found a big treasure yet," said Grandma, "but we've acquired many small, valuable things."

At the bottom of the Korean box lay another poem.

> Look still further, my dear friend.
> The treasure hunt's not at an end.
> Go to where my coats do stay.
> This will lead you on your way.
> Look in! Look on!
> Look above! Look below!
> You will turn something
> Then you will know.

We raced to the hall closet. Dad, being the tallest, swept everything off the shelves. Grandma pulled out the few coats and searched in the pockets. Mom, Jacob, and I went through the boxes, boots, umbrellas, and bags on the floor of the closet.

"Nothing in here," I grumbled.

"We haven't found anything that turns," Mom said as she shut the closet door. "Ooooh! I said that at the very same time I was turning this big wooden doorknob!" exclaimed Mom.

© Houghton Mifflin Harcourt Publishing Company

Jacob dashed off to find a screwdriver. In no time, my handy little brother had removed the whole knob.

Grandma was the one who discovered that the knob was made up of two parts. She and Dad tugged in opposite directions until the wooden ball separated.

Out fell an emerald ring and still another one of those puzzling rhymes.

You've come so far
With each clue,
Yet you still haven't found
The best treasure for you.

Search for an object
That has something to tell.
If you can find it,
You'll be rewarded well.

It's on a place where
I've spend some time
Paying my bills
Or writing a rhyme.

Look it over,
Then get it to the rear.
Don't give up!
Just please persevere!

Dad said, "Naturally, the place where she wrote rhymes and checks would be at one of these desks. But which one?"

"We searched through all three of them, and we didn't find anything," I recalled. There we were, just where we had started, staring at three antique desks.

Again we pushed on carved parts. We pulled knobs, doors, and moldings. We tapped, rapped, banged, and knocked.

"It's fun to have a treasure hunt," said Jacob, "but it's upsetting when it takes so long!"

"We must persevere, just as Marge's rhyme said," warned Grandma.

I mumbled, "I'm not fond of any of this furniture, but this bedroom desk is positively the worst. It's so ugly with that clock built into the top. The clock doesn't even tick anymore. It's always 1:38." I stopped. A clock can tell something—time! I thought of the rhyme. Search for a place that has something to tell. Hunt in the rear. I shrieked! Dad was following my thoughts. He rushed for a ladder. I climbed up and tried to open the rear of the clock. I pulled on the cover, but it refused to budge.

© Houghton Mifflin Harcourt Publishing Company

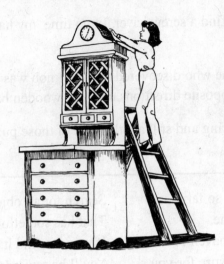

"Press all the fancy carved flowers and leaves," said Grandma. "Maybe there's a hidden button that will open the clock."

I was so excited I almost fell off the ladder. I let Grandma take my place. She leaned her hand for balance on a design in the wood. Click. The clock swung out! Behind it were three drawers. In the center drawer was an old-fashioned cassette tape.

"I'll go look for a cassette player so we can listen to this," Dad said.

The air was thick with excitement, as they say in books. What fun it was to solve a mystery!

While we waited for Dad to come back, the four of us stood in front of a painting on a wall. It seemed to have enchanted all of us.

"This is really lovely!" Mom exclaimed to Grandma. "If you don't want this painting, please let us have it."

"I think it's beautiful, too," Grandma remarked.

The painting was of a woman in a yellow silk jacket trimmed in white fur. She was standing near a window, arranging a bowl of flowers. Sunlight poured in the window onto the flowers, the woman, and her clothes. The room behind her was in shadow. We could see an old map on the wall and a table covered with a heavy oriental rug. But the lovely light on the scene made the colors glow.

Jacob spoke up. "I'm usually bored when we go to museums. But there's something about this picture that makes me want to stare at it."

Everyone was agreeing with him just as Dad walked into the room holding a cassette player. A few seconds later, Mrs. McIntosh's voice rang out. What she said astonished us!

© Houghton Mifflin Harcourt Publishing Company
Core Skills Reading Comprehension, Grade 6

> You have found it, my friend, Faye!
> You're great with puzzles, I always did say.
> Here's a priceless painting—yours to keep;
> So are the furnishings and every antique.
> This lovely picture is worth the most;
> Of its beauty you can certainly boast.
> Enjoy the colors, the figure serene—
> It's the work of an artist not often seen.

"Here we were just admiring this painting," exclaimed Grandma, "and it turns out to be the great treasure!"

"It can't be that valuable," said Dad.

"Maybe something is hidden behind the picture," suggested Mom.

Dad lifted the painting from the wall. Seen at even closer range, the painting appeared to be quite old. The paint had tiny cracks in it. Dad cautiously removed the frame and the backing. Nothing was concealed either behind the picture or in the frame. No one said a word.

"It's obvious that we have a treasure," Grandma said, "but what is it? . . . Oh, well. I know that the greatest treasure I received was the pleasure of working together with my family."

I was about to express my disappointment. But when I saw Grandma's face, I decided not to. After all, the hunt for Mrs. McIntosh's treasure *had* been fun.

Later, when Belinda was back at her house, she decided to do some detective work to discover more about the beautiful painting. Yet she didn't know where to start. She thought she might talk with some experts. But she was afraid that people who were famous experts on paintings wouldn't take time from their busy schedules to speak to a girl. Finally, Belinda prepared this list of other possible experts.

© Houghton Mifflin Harcourt Publishing Company

Name _____ Date _____

Possible Experts

an art teacher in school

a friend who is taking art lessons

the man in the paint and wallpaper shop

the director of the city museum

the man who owns the art supply shop

a neighbor who collects oil paintings

the head librarian of the art library

---

1. Name the four experts you think might help Belinda the most.

a. _____

b. _____

c. _____

d. _____

2. In what order would you advise Belinda to go to these experts to discuss the painting? Start with the ones most likely to know more about painting. Write them on these lines.

a. _____

b. _____

c. _____

d. _____

© Houghton Mifflin Harcourt Publishing Company

The experts listened to Belinda's description. They looked at photographs that she had taken of the painting. Almost all of the experts had suggestions about artists who could have painted it. But without expensive testing, the experts couldn't be certain. All of them told Belinda to check out their hints in other places.

The experts suggested she look for the following:

- artists who had lived in the 1500s, 1600s, or 1700s, judging by the woman's clothing
- artists from Belgium and Holland because the room in the background looked like one that might have existed in those countries during certain time periods
- oil paintings

Belinda used a set of encyclopedias to look up information about the artists the experts had mentioned. In which volumes should she look?

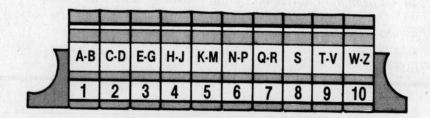

B **Think of topics Belinda could look up. Write the information on the lines below. Use the headings given.**

Volume	Letters	Topic
1. _____	_____	_____
2. _____	_____	_____
3. _____	_____	_____
4. _____	_____	_____
5. _____	_____	_____

© Houghton Mifflin Harcourt Publishing Company

C Here is a list of art books Belinda looked at. Write five titles that might include the works of Belgian or Dutch artists who worked in the years from 1500 until 1750.

Art Books

Art in America

The Best of French Artists: 1500–1800

European Art and Artists

A Guide to European Painters

Famous Artists and Their Works

Great Names in Art from the Fourteenth Century to the Seventeenth Century

Children of Famous Painters

Great Masterpieces of Belgium

---

1. _____

2. _____

3. _____

4. _____

5. _____

Art books contain many photographs of paintings. Belinda wanted to narrow her search to include only works by artists of the correct period and country. Of these, she wanted to read about artists who painted pictures of women inside a home. She wanted to examine works only of the possible artists who specialized in pale, beautiful colors gleaming in sunlight. She also remembered Mrs. McIntosh's words that this painter's work was seldom seen.

Prepared with these clues, she tackled some thick art books. Because the table of contents in each of them provided only general information and she didn't want to read whole chapters, Belinda decided to use the index. Here are some things Belinda had learned about indexes.

---

1. The index is always at the end of the book.

2. The index is arranged in alphabetical order.

3. The index tells what topics are included in the book.

4. The index tells how much information can be found on the topic.

5. The index tells on which pages the information in located.

6. The index, like an outline, organizes the information under **main ideas**, **subtopics**, and **details**.

© Houghton Mifflin Harcourt Publishing Company

D Here is a part of an index from an art book. Study it and then answer the questions.

Ancient Art, 6, 9, 14, 35–270, 422–428;
    Byzantine, 35–41;
    cave drawings, 6, 9;
    early Christian, 14, 103–142, 422–428;
    Egyptian, 42–83, 85–98;
    Greek, 40–83, 85–98;
    Roman, 9, 84, 85, 98–142;
Medieval art (years 900–1250), 307–637;
    architecture, 307–461;
      castles, 307, 311, 312–350;
      churches, 103–145, 308, 351–383;
    glass, stained, 422–426;
      illustration, 424;
    religious art, 360–475, 490–493;
    sculpture, 495–520;
      illustrations, 499, 518;

Renaissance art (years 1300–1700), 638–1058;
    Dutch, see Netherlands;
    England, 828–1018;
      painting, 866–893, 895, 899–910;
        illustrations, 870, 891, 900–905;
    Flemish, see Netherlands;
    Italy, 638–820;
      architecture, 602–620;
      murals, 811, 813, 815–820;
      painting, 684–691, 798;
      sculpture, 720–814, 819;
    Netherlands, 1062–1132;
      architecture, 1062–1132;
      map, 1063;
      painting, 1089–1132;

1. Which pages have information on medieval art? _____

2. Which pages have information on ancient Greek art?

   _____

3. The period of Renaissance art is considered by this index to include which years?

   _____

4. Give all the pages that have information about sculpture.

   _____

5. If Belinda doesn't find the information she needs in this book, what should she do? Circle the correct answer.

   a. look in the glossary

   b. look in the index of another art book

   c. look in the table of contents of a book on a sculpture

   d. search in the dictionary

© Houghton Mifflin Harcourt Publishing Company

After her research, Belinda was sure that the painting looked like the work of either of two Dutch artists from the 1600s. Whether it was real or a fake, she had no way of knowing.

But a few months later, there was a notice in the paper. A famous art museum was sending some experts to Belinda's city. They would examine paintings to decide if they were valuable.

When the experts saw Grandma's painting, they knew it was rare and valuable. There was a mark at the bottom that the family hadn't noticed. That was one of the ways the artist had signed his pictures. So, in the end, Grandma had inherited a valuable treasure from her good friend Mrs. McIntosh!

E Work out the acrostic puzzle using the clues. The letters down the center will spell out the identity of a famous painter.

wearily	search	budge	concealed	ivory	trek
priceless	suspense	obvious	tiresome	exclaim	antique
jade	shriek	persevere	grumble	object	oriental
acquire	hideous	tentacle			

1. a kind of valuable stone

2. to move slightly

3. to walk for a long time

4. to cry out

5. very ugly

6. in a tired way

7. to keep on trying

8. an "arm" of an octopus

9. to gain possession of

10. nervousness caused by wondering what will happen

11. very old

12. a thing

13. to hunt or look for

14. hidden

15. plain to see

16. to scream or yell

17. the material an elephant's tusks are made of

18. to complain

19. a type of rug from Asia

20. causing a person to feel impatient or bored

21. having a value that is more than any possible price

© Houghton Mifflin Harcourt Publishing Company

1. ___ ___ ___ ___

2. ___ ___ ___ ___

3. ___ ___ ___ ___

4. ___ ___ ___ ___

5. ___ ___ ___ ___

6. ___ ___ ___ ___

7. ___ ___ ___ ___

8. ___ ___ ___ ___

9. ___ ___ ___ ___

10. ___ ___ ___ ___

11. ___ ___ ___ ___

12. ___ ___ ___ ___

13. ___ ___ ___ ___

14. ___ ___ ___ ___ ___

15. ___ ___ ___

16. ___ ___ ___ ___

17. ___ ___ ___ ___

18. ___ ___ ___ ___

19. ___ ___ ___ ___

20. ___ ___ ___ ___

21. ___ ___ ___

39

Selection 6: Paired

Frederick Douglass: Abolitionist Leader

Though he was born into slavery, Frederick Douglass (1818?–1895) educated himself and became one of the greatest speakers and writers in the United States. He worked most of his adult life to abolish, or bring an end to, slavery, racism, and the unequal treatment of women. His life was an inspiration to others struggling for civil rights.

Frederick Douglass's name at birth was Frederick Bailey. He was born into slavery. As a boy, he heard his master say that a black person with an education could never be kept as a slave. From early on, Frederick wanted to learn to read and write. At not even ten years old, he knew it was the only way he could hope to escape the bonds of slavery.

He had been born in Talbot County, Maryland. His mother died when he was young. The boy was treated badly by the slave owner. Later, he was shipped off to live with another member of the owner's family in Baltimore, Maryland.

His new master, Hugh Auld, was like most slave owners. He wanted to make sure Frederick was kept ignorant. Auld's wife Sophia, however, was kind. She tried to teach Frederick simple spelling and reading. She also put him in charge of their son, Thomas. Auld commanded his wife to stop teaching Frederick to read. He said it would make the boy dangerous.

A VOICE FROM THE PAST

From that moment I understood the pathway from slavery to freedom. It was just what I wanted and I got it at a time when I least expected it. Whilst I was saddened by the thought of losing the aid of my kind mistress, I was gladdened by the invaluable instruction which, by the merest accident, I had gained from my master.

FREDERICK DOUGLASS, quoted in *Escape from Slavery*

Role Model Even though Frederick knew it would be difficult to learn without a teacher, he was determined. Each time he was left alone, he would look for a book or newspaper. He would do his best to figure out the words and their meanings. If education was the way out of slavery, he knew he did not have a moment to waste.

He started attending the Bible classes taught by a free black man named Dr. Lewis G. Wells. Soon, Frederick was reading from the Bible and teaching other slaves how God had saved the Hebrews in Egypt from the evil Pharaoh. Dr. Wells said that just as God had used Moses, He was going to use Frederick to set his people free.

© Houghton Mifflin Harcourt Publishing Company

Frederick's master became concerned about what Frederick was learning at church. He sent him back to the plantation to work as a field slave. On the plantation, a white supervisor beat Frederick to teach him to fear whites. Risking his life, Frederick fought the supervisor to show him that he was unwilling to be treated so badly. Frederick later said the event was a turning point in his life. He knew he had the courage to be free.

New Name   Frederick was soon trying to convince other slaves to run away. When the slave owners in the area learned of the plan, they demanded that Frederick be sold or sent elsewhere. He was shipped back to Baltimore, where he had first learned to read. There, he was put to work on the ship docks. In 1838, he made his escape to New York, where slavery was not permitted. He knew he had to change his last name to escape the men who were pursuing him because he had run away. He finally settled on Douglass as his new name. He chose it because Douglass was a character in a popular poem, *The Lady of the Lake*, by Sir Walter Scott.

For three years Frederick Douglass worked at various odd jobs. He was proud to earn money and not be forced to give it to his master. He also married Anna Murray. And it was during this time that he met William Lloyd Garrison, publisher of the antislavery newspaper titled *The Liberator*.

A VOICE FROM THE PAST

The [news]paper became my meat and my drink. My soul was set all on fire. Its sympathy for my brethren in bonds—its scathing denunciations of slaveholders—its faithful exposures of slavery—and its powerful attacks upon the upholders of the institution—sent a thrill of joy through my soul, such as I had never felt before!

FREDERICK DOUGLASS, *The Narrative of the Life of Frederick Douglass,*
An American Slave

Spokesman and Writer   By 1841, Frederick Douglass was not just reading *The Liberator*. He was also writing articles for it. Garrison was impressed with Douglass. He encouraged him to share his story so the world could hear just how horrible slavery was. His dynamic talents proved to the world what black people could accomplish, if they were given the chance.

In 1847, Douglass started his own abolitionist newspaper, *The North Star*, in Rochester, New York. In addition, he risked his life to help runaway slaves who came through New York on their way to Canada on the Underground Railroad. However, he was not simply interested in helping black people. He became a spokesperson for women's rights as well.

© Houghton Mifflin Harcourt Publishing Company

The Civil War broke out in 1861. Douglass used his speaking talents to recruit blacks to join the Federal Army, the army of the Northern states. When he saw how poorly the black soldiers were treated, he went straight to President Abraham Lincoln with his complaint. The president told Douglass that the fight for civil rights would be a slow one and that he must be patient.

End of Slavery In March of 1865, Frederick Douglass was invited to the White House to help celebrate Lincoln's re-election. When he first appeared, the guards would not let him in because he was black. Even in Lincoln's White House, it was a slow process to change people's prejudices.

A month later, the Civil War was over. The Confederate Army had surrendered. As Federal troops swept through the South, they freed millions of slaves from their masters. But in the midst of Douglass's joy over the end of slavery, tragic news reached him: On April 14, 1865, John Wilkes Booth had shot and killed Lincoln.

After the Civil War, opportunities for blacks slowly increased. In 1877, Douglass was named a United States marshal, and in 1881 he was appointed recorder of deeds for the city of Washington, DC. By the end of the decade, he was named ambassador to Haiti. Douglass also made a trip to Egypt, the land that had first inspired him to fight against slavery when he read stories from the Bible.

For the rest of his life, Douglass spoke and wrote about the evils of racism. On February 20, 1895, after attending a rally for women's rights, Douglass returned to his hotel room. While recalling the day's speeches, Douglass suddenly fell to the floor. The great man was dead of natural causes at age 77.

42

Ⓐ **Circle the correct answer for each question.**

1. Who was the first person to teach Frederick to read?

   a. Dr. Louis G. Wells

   b. the wife of his second master

   c. his first master

   d. a boy in his Baltimore neighborhood

2. Look at the heading "Role Model." What kind of role model was Douglass?

   a. a role model to show anyone, black or white, that he or she could learn to read

   b. a role model to show slaves that they could attempt to escape slavery

   c. a role model to show white supervisors that slaves would work better with kinder treatment

   d. a role model to show people at the church that they could lead black people out of slavery

3. What is the first paragraph in the section titled "New Name" *mostly* about?

   a. Douglass's work on the ship docks

   b. Douglass's name change

   c. Douglass's escape from slavery

   d. Douglass's return to Baltimore

4. What are two specific actions that Douglass took that involved him risking his life?

   a. Douglass fought with a white supervisor, and later he helped runaway slaves escape to Canada.

   b. Douglass learned to read and write, and later he wrote articles for *The Liberator* newspaper.

   c. Douglass encouraged blacks to join the Federal Army, and later he met with President Lincoln to discuss their treatment.

   d. Douglass shared his story of having been a slave, and later he became a spokesperson for women's rights.

5. When did Frederick realize that he had gained the courage to be free from slavery?

   a. when he escaped to New York

   b. when he started reading the Bible

   c. when he first began to read in Baltimore

   d. when he fought a white supervisor on a plantation

43

6. Which fact supports the idea that Frederick Douglass used his skills to protest slavery?

   a. In 1877, Douglass was named a United States marshal.

   b. In 1865, Douglass was invited to the White House.

   c. In 1847, Douglass started his own abolitionist newspaper.

   d. In the 1830s, Douglass worked on ship docks in Baltimore.

7. Which of these can the reader conclude based on information in the selection?

   a. Douglass was uncertain that President Abraham Lincoln should have been re-elected.

   b. Douglass felt that blacks should not have fought in the Civil War.

   c. Douglass had dreamed of writing for a newspaper long before he did it.

   d. Douglass traveled to places outside the United States.

8. What is meant by the word *bonds* in this selection?

   a. a type of financial investment

   b. a type of agreement

   c. a type of captivity

   d. a type of glue

9. How did the author organize the selection?

   a. The author began with general information about the Civil War and then described specific information about Frederick Douglass.

   b. The author told events in Frederick Douglass's life in chronological order.

   c. The author described the problem of slavery and then explained what Frederick Douglass did to help solve the problem.

   d. The author compared and contrasted Frederick Douglass with William Lloyd Garrison.

10. The tone of this selection encourages readers to

    a. be more sympathetic to the views of Northern states during the Civil War.

    b. comprehend that public opinion on racism changed after the Civil War.

    c. understand the effectiveness of political speeches.

    d. view slavery as a terrible institution.

11. Which quotation from the passage *best* expresses the author's positive view of Douglass as an important historical figure?

    a. *His dynamic talents proved to the world what black people could accomplish, if they were given the chance.*

    b. *But in the midst of Douglass's joy over the end of slavery, tragic news reached him.*

    c. *He was shipped back to Baltimore, where he had first learned to read.*

    d. *When he saw how poorly the black soldiers were treated, he went straight to President Abraham Lincoln with his complaint.*

© Houghton Mifflin Harcourt Publishing Company

Name _____ Date _____

B **Answer the questions on the lines provided.**

1. Why did Frederick change his last name?

   _____

   _____

2. Explain how the author introduces the important theme of "escaping the bonds of slavery" in the selection.

   _____

   _____

   _____

3. What do the features titled "A Voice from the Past" contribute to the selection?

   _____

   _____

   _____

© Houghton Mifflin Harcourt Publishing Company

C **Match the correct effect to its cause. Write the letter of the effect beside the cause.**

<table>
<tr><th>CAUSE</th><th>EFFECT</th></tr>
<tr><td>_____ 1. Because slavery was not permitted there,</td><td>a. Douglass was overwhelmed by grief when the president was killed.</td></tr>
<tr><td>_____ 2. Because Hugh Auld wanted to keep all slaves ignorant,</td><td>b. Hugh Auld sent him away to work on a plantation.</td></tr>
<tr><td>_____ 3. Because Douglass did not agree with how black soldiers were being treated,</td><td>c. he was sent to Baltimore and forced to work on ship docks.</td></tr>
<tr><td>_____ 4. Because he loved President Lincoln for having freed slaves,</td><td>d. Douglass ran away to New York.</td></tr>
<tr><td>_____ 5. Because The Liberator exposed the horrors of slavery,</td><td>e Douglass was thrilled to write articles for it.</td></tr>
<tr><td>_____ 6. Because President Lincoln knew that the struggle for civil rights would be slow,</td><td>f. Douglass learned to read and write.</td></tr>
<tr><td>_____ 7. Because Douglass was learning about setting people free,</td><td>g. he traveled there.</td></tr>
<tr><td>_____ 8. Because the land of Egypt had inspired Douglass as a boy to fight against slavery,</td><td>h. he told Douglass to be patient.</td></tr>
<tr><td>_____ 9. Because Douglass was encouraging plantation slaves to run away,</td><td>i. he told his wife to stop teaching Douglass to spell and read.</td></tr>
<tr><td>_____ 10. Because he had learned that education was the way out of slavery,</td><td>j. he met with the president to complain.</td></tr>
</table>

© Houghton Mifflin Harcourt Publishing Company

Selection 7: Paired

Narrative of the Life of Frederick Douglass, an American Slave
—excerpt from Chapter 7

I lived in Master Hugh's family about seven years. During this time, I succeeded in learning to read and write. In accomplishing this, I was compelled to resort to various strategems. I had no regular teacher. . . .

The plan which I adopted, and the one by which I was most successful, was that of making friends of all the little white boys whom I met in the street. As many of these as I could, I converted into teachers. With their kindly aid, obtained at different times and in different places, I finally succeeded in learning to read. When I was sent of errands, I always took my book with me, and by going one part of my errand quickly, I found time to get a lesson before my return. I used also to carry bread with me, enough of which was always in the house, and to which I was always welcome; for I was much better off in this regard than many of the poor white children in our neighborhood. This bread I used to bestow on the hungry little urchins, who, in return, would give me that more valuable bread of knowledge. I am strongly tempted to give the names of two or three of those little boys, as a testimonial of the gratitude and affection I bear them; but prudence forbids;—not that it would injure me, but it might embarrass them; for it is almost an unpardonable offence[1] to teach slaves to read in this Christian country. It is enough to say of the dear little fellows, that they lived on Philpot Street, very near Durgin and Bailey's shipyard. I used to talk this matter of slavery over with them. I would sometimes say to them, I wished I could be as free as they would be when they got to be men. "You will be free as soon as you are twenty-one, *but I am a slave for life*! Have not I as good a right to be free as you have?" These words used to trouble them; they would express for me the liveliest sympathy, and console me with the hope that something would occur by which I might be free.

I was now about twelve years old, and the thought of being *a slave for life* began to bear heavily upon my heart.

[1] **offence:** the modern American English spelling is *offense*

A Circle the correct answer for each question.

1. Read this sentence from the first paragraph.

> In accomplishing this, I was compelled to resort
> to various strategems. I had no regular teacher. . . .

Which word in the first sentence of the next paragraph helps the reader understand what *strategems* means?

a. *plan*   **b.** *boys*   **c.** *successful*   **d.** *friends*

2. In what way was Frederick Douglass better off than some of the poor white children in his neighborhood?

   a. He wore better clothes.

   b. He was given the freedom to do errands.

   c. He had more food to eat.

   d. He was treated better at home.

3. When would Douglass find time to get in a reading lesson?

   a. when he was playing with boys in his neighborhood

   b. when he was running an errand

   c. when he was in Master Hugh's house

   d. when he was at Durgin and Bailey's shipyard

4. Which of these words *best* describes how Douglass felt about the boys in his neighborhood?

   a. inferior

   b. superior

   c. thankful

   d. jealous

5. Referring to the poor boys in his neighborhood, Douglass said that "As many of these as I could, I converted into teachers." Which of the following *best* supports this claim?

   a. He made friends with "all the little white boys" he met in the street.

   b. There was more food available to him than to the "poor white children" in his neighborhood.

   c. He was tempted to name a few of the boys in his writing, as a "testimonial of the gratitude and affection" he felt toward them.

   d. The boys gave him the "more valuable bread of knowledge."

6. Which of these details creates a break in the narrative?

   a. Douglass said that he would like to mention the names of the boys who helped him with reading lessons.

   b. Douglass said that he came up with a plan to make friends with all the boys he met in the street.

   c. Douglass said that he did errands quickly so that he could get in a lesson before he was expected home again.

   d. Douglass said that he sometimes reminded the boys in his neighborhood that he would be a slave the rest of his life.

© Houghton Mifflin Harcourt Publishing Company
Core Skills Reading Comprehension, Grade 6

B **Answer the questions on the lines provided.**

1. Why did Douglass give bread to boys in his neighborhood?

_____

_____

_____

2. Write a summary of this selection.

_____

_____

_____

C **Choose a word from below to complete each sentence.**

bestow	accomplish	convert	compelled
urchin	gratitude	tempted	testimonial
prudence	offense	unpardonable	console

1. To change someone into something else is to _____.

2. A sense of cautiousness is _____.

3. To make someone feel better emotionally is to _____.

4. To present as a gift is to _____.

5. To succeed at doing something is to _____.

6. A child who is poor and dressed in rags is an _____.

7. To be forced to do something is to be _____.

8. Something that is unforgivable is _____.

9. To risk the dangers of doing something is to be _____.

10. An act of breaking the law or breaking a moral code is an _____.

11. A statement that praises someone is a _____.

12. To show that you are thankful is to show _____.

49

© Houghton Mifflin Harcourt Publishing Company

A metaphor is a figure of speech in which two unlike things are compared because they surprisingly have something in common. Think about the following sentence.

> Frederick Douglass was determined to break through the solid walls of slavery that surrounded and confined him.

At first, you might think that walls and slavery have nothing in common. A wall is something you can touch. You can't touch slavery—it's an idea. But what do slavery and a wall have in common? If a person is completely surrounded by walls and can't get out, then the walls restrict that person's freedom. Slavery would, too—in a very different way.

Here are more metaphors.

My mom the tornado swept through the house and had it cleaned in no time.

"Time was a thief," said my grandfather, "robbing me too quickly of my youth."

Life is a long, wonderful, challenging journey.

D **Respond to each item on the lines provided.**

1. Frederick Douglass said that the boys in his neighborhood gave him "that more valuable bread of knowledge." Explain why "bread of knowledge" is a metaphor. *Hint:* Think about what "bread" and "knowledge" would seem to have in common for Douglass.

   _____

   _____

   _____

2. In another part of Douglass's autobiography, he described the abolitionist newspaper, called *The Liberator*, for which he wrote articles. He said, "The [news]paper became my meat and my drink." Explain why this is a metaphor.

   _____

   _____

   _____

© Houghton Mifflin Harcourt Publishing Company

For each pair of words, write a sentence with a metaphor that uses the two words given.

3. eyes, camera

_____

4. hair, snakes

_____

5. mountains, curtains

_____

6. music, shield

_____

Now write a sentence with a metaphor that uses two words of your own choosing.

7. _____

E **Think about the excerpt from Frederick Douglass's autobiography and about "Frederick Douglass: Abolitionist Leader." Respond to each item on the lines provided.**

1. In the excerpt from his autobiography, Douglass said that he had "no regular teacher" when it came to learning to read. Using details from both selections, explain the reason for this.

_____

_____

_____

_____

2. Use details from both selections to compare the boys in Frederick Douglass's Baltimore neighborhood with his two masters.

_____

_____

_____

_____

51

3. Think about how Frederick Douglass learned to read and who helped him.

    a. Name one fact about this that is presented in the excerpt from Douglass's autobiography that is not presented in "Frederick Douglass: Abolitionist Leader."

_____

_____

    b. Name two facts about this that are presented in "Frederick Douglass: Abolitionist Leader" that are not presented in the excerpt from Douglass's autobiography.

_____

_____

_____

_____

4. Think about the way the author organized "Frederick Douglass: Abolitionist Leader." The excerpt from Douglass's autobiography is organized in a different way. Explain the difference.

_____

_____

_____

5. Compare Frederick Douglass's most likely purpose for writing his autobiography with the author's most likely purpose for writing "Frederick Douglass: Abolitionist Leader."

_____

_____

_____

52

© Houghton Mifflin Harcourt Publishing Company

6. The *tone* of a text is the attitude the writer takes toward a character, toward the audience, or toward the subject of the work. Contrast the tone of "Frederick Douglass: Abolitionist Leader" with the tone of Douglass's autobiography. Explain your choice of words to describe the tone of each selection.

_____

_____

_____

_____

_____

7. Which of the two selections did you enjoy reading more? Why?

_____

_____

_____

_____

© Houghton Mifflin Harcourt Publishing Company

Skills Review: Selections 1–7

A Hyperbole is a figure of speech that uses an incredible exaggeration. A writer may use hyperbole to create humor or to make a character or event seem impressive to readers. Put a ✓ in front of each example of hyperbole.

_____ 1. There were a million books in Mrs. McIntosh's house—on bookshelves, in closets, on tables, and on the floor.

_____ 2. Jacob ran so fast to go find a screwdriver that his feet stopped touching the floor.

_____ 3. Belinda felt disgusted at the little ivory statue of the horrid-looking rat.

_____ 4. Mom was so tired that she couldn't take another minute of the search for the treasure.

_____ 5. When the two parts of the wooden doorknob finally came apart, Dad and Grandma had been tugging so hard that they were both flung to opposite ends of the apartment.

_____ 6. The colors in the painting were so brilliant that they blinded Belinda.

_____ 7. Mrs. McIntosh's confusing rhymes made Jacob want to cry in frustration.

_____ 8. The gold earrings sparkled in the sunshine that was streaming through a nearby window.

B An idiom is a word or phrase that means something different from the literal meaning of each word. Read the following items. For each one, underline the idiom and then write the letter of the meaning of the idiom in the blank before the number.

_____ 1. Jacob finally got tired of trying to figure out Mrs. McIntosh's rhymes. "I wish she would stop beating around the bush."

_____ 2. Mrs. McIntosh knew antiques backward and forward. That is why Grandma used to ask her for information about old clocks.

_____ 3. On the third day of the hunt for the treasure, Belinda pounded the table with impatience. "Don't get bent out of shape," Dad told her. "A treasure hunt takes time."

_____ 4. Grandma said, "I always used to get a kick out of Marge's excitement whenever she located another tiny jade figure."

_____ 5. Mr. Boaz, the lawyer, would have liked to help Grandma solve the mystery. But he had his hands full with legal cases.

a. was busy   **b.** thoroughly   **c.** enjoy   **d.** angry   **e.** wasting time

© Houghton Mifflin Harcourt Publishing Company

C Complete each sentence by circling the correct word. Remember to think about how the things compare or relate to each other.

1. *Pencil* is to *write* as *truck* is to _____.

   kiss   wheel   drive

2. *Lungs* are to *people* as *gills* are to _____.

   monkeys   insects   fish

3. *Clue* is to *hint* as *odor* is to _____.

   scent   cent   food

4. *Humid* is to *jungle* as *dry* is to _____.

   mountain   desert   valley

5. *Nephew* is to *niece* as *uncle* is to _____.

   cousin   aunt   sister

D Some words have more than one meaning and pronunciation. Study the word below, its pronunciations, and its meanings. Then write the letter of the correct meaning of the word next to each sentence.

object: a. (ob′ ject)   *n:* a purpose, an aim, an end
          b. (ob′ ject)   *n:* a thing; a person
          c. (ob ject′)   *v:* to oppose; to protest against

_____ 1. They *objected* to people walking across their lawn.

_____ 2. The *object* of the game was to score touchdowns.

_____ 3. The *object* of the project was to complete it in three weeks.

_____ 4. The hero was the *object* of everyone's admiration.

_____ 5. The teacher *objects* to having the students call out.

_____ 6. Improving her work in decimals is Angela's *object*.

_____ 7. There was a mysterious *object* in the brook.

_____ 8. The cats were loudly *objecting* to eating the stale food.

© Houghton Mifflin Harcourt Publishing Company

E The tone of a selection or poem is the attitude the writer takes toward a character, toward the audience, or toward the subject of the work. On the line before each paragraph, write the letter of the word that *best* describes the tone of the writing.

a. urgent

b. exaggerated

c. admiring

d. serene

e. comical

f. informative

g. conversational

h. dreamy

_____ 1.   How much time is left before even more forests are destroyed by wildfires? Based on the events of the past few years, not much! Each summer thousands of acres have burned in the West. Changes in forest management must be made now—before it's too late.

_____ 2.   It was very early in the morning. Binoculars in hand, Caitlin walked noiselessly along the trails in Lancaster Woods. Suddenly she stopped. Could that be a yellow-bellied sapsucker half-hidden in the branches above her? She slowly raised her binoculars to her eyes, anticipating a beautiful sight.

_____ 3.   My great-grandfather, Ernest Baeza, had joined the army when he was eighteen years old. Yet, despite how young he was, he was awarded three medals for bravery during World War II. He didn't seem to know the meaning of the word *fear*. There was a story behind each of those medals, and each story involved him rescuing a fellow soldier who would have died without my great-grandfather's bravery and help.

_____ 4.   All firefighters in the wilderness are required to have fire shelters clipped to their belt. Fire shelters are flame-retardant bags that can be placed all around the head and body. They are used if a firefighter is surrounded by a blaze. Wearing a fire shelter is like wearing a tent.

_____ 5.   Mr. Krueger had lived next door for decades before Rose was born. Rose had grown up helping Mr. Krueger do things like rake leaves (even when she was too little to move the rake), scrub his front porch (even though she made more of a mess than he actually cleaned), and weed his garden (even if she often pulled up vegetable plants). When she first learned the word *patient*, she decided that Mr. Krueger was the most patient person in the world.

56

F Here is part of an index from a book about ancient peoples. See if you remember how to locate information in an index. Answer the questions that follow.

Farming,
  Cave people, 5–12, 17–19;
    picture, 8;
  Europe, 126–139;
  Iron Age, 150–159;
  Near East, 166–172;
    maps, 167, 171;
  Origin, 52, 80–87;
  River delta, 36–41;
Hunting,
  Ceremonies, 29;
  Early Egyptians, 34–35, 39;
  Eskimos, 22–27;
  Stone Age, 16, 20–21;
Metalworking,
  Celtic, 54;
  Chinese, 187–189, 193–197, 200;
    picture, 194;
  Etruscan, 125, 198–203;
  Origin, 152, 159;

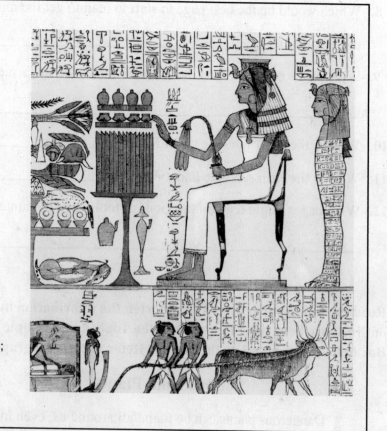

1. On what pages would you look to find out about the kinds of metal objects made by the people of China?

_____

2. How many subtopics are listed for *Hunting*? _____

3. Does this index give any information about laws relating to hunting seasons?

_____

4. Which pages would you read to find the most information about life during the Stone Age?

_____

5. What subtopic would you read to find out when people first began to make objects from metal?

_____

6. On what pages will you find maps of the Near East? _____

© Houghton Mifflin Harcourt Publishing Company

7. Are there more pages of information about farming in early Europe or farming in the Near East?

_____

8. Which would be the best page to start to read to get the most information about metal artwork of

the Etruscans? _____

9. What pages might tell you the kinds of tools used by farmers during the Iron Age?

_____

10. What is the third subtopic under *Hunting*? _____

11. What is the fifth subtopic under *Farming*? _____

12. What pages might tell you the kinds of tools used by hunters during the Stone Age?

_____

G **Read the following article. Then shorten the information by outlining it. Some parts of the outline have been done for you. Use the Topic and Subtopic Box and the Additional Information Box to help you complete the outline. Refer to the paragraphs in the article.**

Poisons from Plants

Dangerous plants can be found all around us, even in our homes. Some of the most popular houseplants are poisonous if the leaves are eaten. Philodendrons, hyacinths, mistletoe, and poinsettias are all poisonous.

There are many poisonous wild plants found in our gardens and lawns. The most common of these are poison ivy, poison sumac, datura, and wild mushrooms.

Poison ivy and poison sumac are found almost everywhere in the United States. Both grow on sand dunes and seashores and in deserts, forests, mountain areas, and damp swamps. All parts of these plants are poisonous. Just touching a part of one can cause blisters, red skin, and itching.

The datura is also called the jimsonweed or thornapple. Any part of this plant may be poisonous if it is crushed. Jimsonweed grows in all different types of climates in Canada, Europe, and the United States. The poison affects the victim's eyesight, causes nervous twitching, and causes the heartbeat to be irregular—to beat too quickly or too weakly. A large quantity of datura usually brings on unconsciousness and then death.

© Houghton Mifflin Harcourt Publishing Company

Eating wild mushrooms is one of the most common types of plant poisonings. It is difficult to tell the harmless, good mushrooms from the poisonous ones, as they often look alike. For that reason, people should eat only mushrooms purchased in stores. Humans are tempted to try the wild ones, however, because they spring up everywhere—in lawns, gardens, woods, parks, and by the sides of the road in North America and Europe. Poisonous mushrooms are dangerous. They cause violent illness and even death.

Main Idea and Subtopic Box	**Additional Information Box**
Leaves poisonous if eaten	All parts poisonous if crushed
The datura plant	Harmless and harmful mushrooms look alike
Poisonous wild plants	Philodendrons
Wild mushrooms	Large quantity causes unconsciousness and death
Poison ivy and poison sumac	Cause blisters, red skin, and itching
	Poinsettias
	Causes nervous twitching

© Houghton Mifflin Harcourt Publishing Company

Poisons from Plants

I. Poisonous plants in our homes

   A. Kinds

      1. _____

      2. Hyacinths

      3. Mistletoe

      4. _____

   B. _____

II. _____

   A. _____

      1. Found almost everywhere

      2. All parts of plant are poisonous

      3. _____

   B. _____

      1. Found in Canada, Europe, and the United States

      2. _____

      3. Affects eyesight

      4. _____

      5. Causes irregular heartbeat

      6. _____

   C. _____

      1. Found almost everywhere about us in North America and Europe

      2. _____

      3. Cause violent illness and death

© Houghton Mifflin Harcourt Publishing Company

Selection 8

Rain Forest Adventure

"Why did I ever think that a trip here would be fun?" exclaimed Amanda Yamamota as she slapped at a huge insect stinging her face.

Her brother Ethan squashed a hairy spider feasting on his leg. He cried out, "We thought exploring a rain forest would be exciting, not deadly!"

Their friend Rosa Ibarra agreed. She said, "Remember how we begged our parents to take us along? How could we have known that the rain forest would be so thick and overgrown with vines and underbrush that it was a jungle?"

"Right. A jungle we would have to chop our way through," said Ethan. "I'd give anything for a path for my tired feet."

Jaime, Rosa's brother, said, "The temperature is about 100 degrees now. And the humidity is high, too." He sighed. "It isn't very comfortable here."

Jaime, Amanda, Rosa, and Ethan were the only kids with the group of scientists searching the rain forest for some special plants. These rare plants had flowers not found anywhere else in the world. The few blossoms that had already been taken to the United States had such an amazing fragrance that perfume made from the petals was the most popular ever sold. Besides that, testing had shown that the flower stems held an unusual liquid—one that could possibly be used to make a medicine for curing a serious disease. The flowers had been named Mysterias. Explorers were combing jungles in various parts of the world to find more of them.

Perfume makers and drug companies had hired the kids' parents to explore an area in a South American rain forest. The scientists hoped to discover a large number of the Mysterias and take them back to the United States.

61

The two families had joined a group of 30 people and 15 burros. They had started their journey on February 1 into a warm, steamy, unfamiliar world. The rain forest was filled with noisy, brightly colored birds and bugs. Because the jungle was so near the equator and at sea level, its climate was hot all year long. The heat, plus the daily rains, made all the plants grow so quickly that it seemed like they were under some wizard's spell!

At the end of each month, a pair of scientists was sent back to the United States. Each pair had reported the group's failure to find any Mysterias. It was now July 23—and almost time to send another disappointing report.

The kids caught up with the search party. Rosa and Jaime's dad suggested that the group stop to cool off in a clear pool they had come upon. Because Jaime was itching from dozens of bug bites, he took out a bar of soap. He was washing himself when he felt a movement close to him.

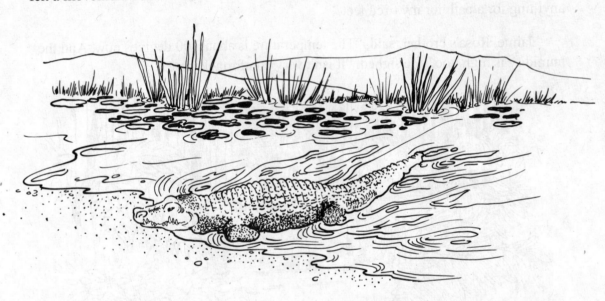

A young crocodile, about three feet long and with its jaws wide open, apparently wanted a taste of Jaime's right leg. "Help!" he shrieked as he scrambled out of the water. "Crocodile! Crocodile!"

In seconds, everyone had gotten out and was standing at the water's edge. The crocodile was left with only a bar of soap. As the group watched, the reptile swallowed it. The last they saw of the creature, it was paddling away in a cloud of bubbles!

Amanda, however, wasn't in the group watching the bubbles. She had run away from the pool to put more distance between her and the crocodile. Not paying attention to anything but getting away, she tripped when her foot caught on a vine on the ground. She fell headfirst into thick underbrush. She lay there stunned for a minute. Finally, she opened her eyes to an odd sight. Some beautiful, pale yellow flowers grew among the bushes. Hundreds of insects circled the blossoms and then landed on them.

© Houghton Mifflin Harcourt Publishing Company

"These flowers really do attract bugs," Amanda thought.

As she watched, the petals suddenly snapped shut, trapping a number of the insects inside. All that could be seen of the flowers now were tight, slender yellow buds.

"Hey!" Amanda called to the others. "I think these flowers eat insects!"

The scientists and the other kids walked over to Amanda to see what had caught her attention. One of the scientists suggested that the group camp there for a few days to make further observations of the flowers.

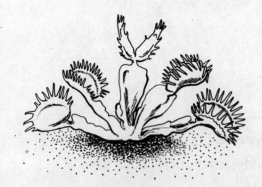

For two days the buds stayed shut. Then on the morning of the third day a similar routine took place. A curious baby monkey heard noises and swung near the flowers. The yellow petals opened. Then one blossom grabbed the little monkey's tail and a tug-of-war followed. The monkey pulled with all its strength to escape, but it was only partly successful. The flower snipped off a tiny piece of the creature's tail. The monkey raced up the nearest tree, screeching.

"It's a meat-eating flower!" exclaimed Dr. Yamamota.

Right away, the scientists made plans to dig up several of the plants. They would be sent back, along with soil, to the United States. Two members of the group and a burro were soon headed back with good news for the first time.

Dr. Ibarra said, "I hope we can grow the plants safely back home. We could use them to kill harmful insects like gyspy moths and fruit flies. Farmers could put the flowers to good use."

Dr. Yamamota said, "But we'll have to make sure they don't destroy helpful insects and small animals."

Another scientist, Dr. Hassan, added, "Though we've made an important discovery thanks to Amanda, we still haven't found the Mysteria plants."

(to be continued)

© Houghton Mifflin Harcourt Publishing Company

A **Circle the correct answer for each question.**

1. What are the first five paragraphs of the selection mainly about?

   a. why the kids had begged their parents to take them to the jungle

   b. what some of the insects looked like that the kids saw

   c. why the kids were not happy being in the jungle

   d. what the jungle looked like to the kids

2. What was a direct effect of Amanda's tripping on a vine?

   a. She dug up a few meat-eating plants and some soil.

   b. She ran to get away from the young crocodile.

   c. She saw part of a monkey's tail get snipped off.

   d. She discovered meat-eating plants.

3. Why are the sixth and seventh paragraphs important to the selection?

   a. They describe the fragrance and appearance of the Mysterias.

   b. They tell what the group of scientists will do with the Mysterias after finding them.

   c. They explain how special plants can be helpful to people who have a serious disease.

   d. They tell the reader why the kids and their parents are in the rain forest.

4. Why does the author mention a wizard?

   a. to give a make-believe quality to the selection

   b. to help the reader understand the effects of the weather in the rain forest

   c. to hint at a wizard who will appear as a character later in the selection

   d. to help the reader understand why the kids thought the rain forest seemed almost magical

© Houghton Mifflin Harcourt Publishing Company

B Details in a selection tell where, when, why, how, who, and what about the topic and/or the action. Skim the selection to find these details or facts. Write the key words that help you locate the information and then answer the questions. One is done for you.

1. Who were the four kids? _kids—Jaime, Amanda, Rosa, and Ethan_

2. What color were the flowers of the meat-eating plant? _____

_____

3. What two things were involved in a tug-of-war? _____

_____

4. What did Ethan squash? _____

5. Who did the small crocodile almost bite? _____

C Where does this selection take place? Where is the rain forest? Skim the selection and look at the map. Then answer the following questions.

1. The rain forest is located close to the _____.

2. On which continent labeled on the map is the rain forest located? _____

3. From which country had the explorers come? _____

4. On which continent labeled on the map is their country located? _____

5. In which direction did the explorers travel from their country to get to the rain forest?

_____

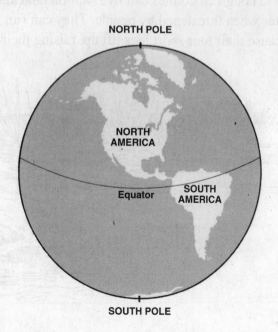

65

D Answer these questions by looking at the map on the previous page and skimming the selection. Underline the correct answer or write the answer for each question.

1. Most places located closer to the equator are (colder, hotter).

2. As you move away from the equator, the weather usually becomes (cooler, warmer).

3. The lower the temperature, the (colder, hotter) it is.

4. The higher the temperature, the (cooler, warmer) it is.

5. The North Pole and the South Pole are as far away as possible from the equator. The South Pole has (cool, very cold, warm, very hot) weather all year long.

6. Most rain forests are located (near, far from) the equator.

7. Most rain forests are (cold, hot) and have (high, low) humidity.

8. In which direction will the explorers travel to take the Mysterias home?

_____

E Read the selection about crocodiles. Use the selection to complete the activity that follows. Write true if the detail is true. Write false if the detail is not true.

Crocodiles

Crocodiles, like other reptiles, have tough, scaly skin that protects them from enemies. Even their stomach is covered with hard scales. Crocodiles have long, powerful tails that they can swing around quickly. One slap from this tail can knock over a large animal.

Though crocodiles can live well on land and in the water, they hide under the water when threatened by people. They can run fast on land for short distances because their four short legs lift up, raising their stomachs off the ground.

© Houghton Mifflin Harcourt Publishing Company

The feet are webbed to enable the animal to paddle about and to help keep its balance in shallow water and mud. The crocodile wiggles its tail from side to side to steer itself when swimming. At that time, all four feet are pressed tightly against its sides, and it zooms along in the water.

The crocodile's nostrils are on top of its nose in the front of its long head. Air is inhaled through the nostrils. Its eyes are set farther back on the head to fool its prey. Sometimes the eyes and the nostrils are kept elevated above the water line with the rest of the head below. In this way, the crocodile lies unnoticed by other animals coming for a drink of water. Because a crocodile resting in the water is disguised as a log, it even catches unaware animals coming to drink that are quite large. The crocodile, with one swipe of its powerful tail, can stun the beast. Then the reptile grabs the animal and kills it. Amazingly enough, crocodiles have even been known to jump up out of the water to capture birds flying low.

For swimming underwater, the crocodile's muscles close off its nose and ears to keep water out. Clear eyelids like transparent curtains slide across the eyes to protect them from water. A flap of skin at the back of the mouth shuts and keeps water out of the throat. The crocodile stays completely underwater for long periods of time.

Crocodiles have 60 to 80 teeth. When a tooth breaks or wears out, a new one grows. These teeth can grab, bite, and tear meat into smaller pieces. They cannot do what your teeth do: chew. That is why crocodiles swallow their food in large hunks.

_____ 1. Crocodiles seldom run on rocky land. Because of their short legs, their stomach gets scraped on the stones.

_____ 2. A crocodile's body is tough and scaly.

_____ 3. Underwater, eyelids cover a crocodile's eyes and keep it from seeing.

_____ 4. When chasing a fast fish, a crocodile moves its legs quickly in the water.

_____ 5. Crocodiles catch animals sometimes by striking them down with their strong tails.

_____ 6. The only use for the crocodile's tail is as a weapon.

_____ 7. The front teeth of crocodiles perform the task of chewing.

_____ 8. Loss of too many teeth has caused crocodiles to starve.

_____ 9. Crocodiles have been known to leap up to catch a flying bird.

_____ 10. The webbed feet of crocodiles help them swim faster.

_____ 11. Crocodiles can move rapidly on land but only for short distances.

_____ 12. Webbed feet enable a crocodile to balance itself in a swamp.

67

© Houghton Mifflin Harcourt Publishing Company

F **Choose a word from below to complete each sentence.**

journey	jungle	squash	routine
failure	vine	burro	attract
scramble	observed	strength	screech
fragrance	comb	temperature	humidity

1. The heat or coldness of something is its _____.

2. To move up or over something quickly is to _____.

3. A loud cry is a _____.

4. Something watched carefully is _____.

5. The dampness of the air is called _____.

6. A long trip is a _____.

7. A lack of success is a _____.

8. A climbing plant is a _____.

9. To search through an area looking for something is to _____.

10. To make something come close is to _____.

11. A kind of donkey is a _____.

12. An overgrown rain forest is a _____.

13. To smash flat is to _____.

14. Something that is done regularly is a _____.

15. The power in your muscles is called _____.

16. Some flowers give off a pleasant _____.

© Houghton Mifflin Harcourt Publishing Company

Selection 9

Amanda and Rosa saw vibrant reds and yellows flashing through the jungle as a pair of birds flew from tree to vine. The colors were so bright that the girls gasped. They had been waiting for an opportunity like this. *Click* went their cameras. The girls' job was to study this particular bird, which the explorers had discovered. The bird's shape was similar to the North American cardinal's, but its colors made the cardinal seem dull by comparison.

Jaime and Ethan had an even more demanding job. They were observing a black and purple bird that blended in with the shadows. It could scarcely be detected. Ethan was creeping toward a thick tree trunk to get a better look at the bird's nest hidden in a hole in the trunk. He crawled closer and closer. Finally, he held onto the tree, trying to climb up.

At that moment, Rosa glanced his way then froze with fright. "Don't move, Ethan!" she called.

Jaime and Amanda also stopped. The kids' long stay in the jungle had taught them to keep perfectly still in times of danger.

Ethan felt the branch he was holding start to move. Twisted around the branch, its green colors blending in with the leaves, was a gigantic, thick snake! Ethan had touched the snake when he grabbed the branch.

"Quiet!" whispered Jaime. "It's a boa!"

The reptile was as surprised as Ethan. With a rapid movement, it slithered from the tree and wrapped itself around the young explorer.

The kids knew they had to remain still to give the snake a chance to escape.

Jaime said slowly, "I'll go for help." Step by step he inched backward, completely unaware that behind him, hidden by the thick vegetation on the jungle floor, was a pit.

Suddenly one of his feet met with air instead of solid ground. He lost his balance and tumbled. As he went down the pit, the shriek he let out echoed through the jungle, frightening the birds. They squawked and screeched as they flew away. The boa, disturbed by all the noise and commotion, twisted itself slightly more tightly around Ethan's body.

© Houghton Mifflin Harcourt Publishing Company

Rosa and Amanda both turned pale. Jaime had disappeared in the pit, and Ethan was in danger of being squeezed to death. But their jungle training had taught them to think quickly. Rosa stayed by Ethan, whispering to him not to move a muscle. Amanda started off to get help. But she didn't make the same mistake Jaime had made. She moved facing forward, watching every step, and noiselessly. She knew that Ethan's life might depend on her silence.

Amanda hurried to the tents where one of the adults was always on guard. "Hurry!" she cried. "A boa is wrapped around Ethan! And Jaime fell into a pit!"

The emergency team rushed into action. One woman remained to stand guard at the camp in case another of the work teams met some difficulty. All the others took first-aid kits, ropes, and tools and followed Amanda.

When Amanda made a signal to show they were nearing Jaime, everyone became silent. Soon they were within view of Rosa and Ethan. Both of them were scarcely breathing, but only one of them had a boa curled around his shoulders. The seconds dragged by. Finally, no longer sensing any danger, the snake slithered down and into the vines and underbrush.

Everyone let out a sigh of relief and then turned their attention to Ethan. Several people started probing the ground with sticks to locate the pit. In a short time, a scientist named Dr. Stewart called out, "Here it is." The hole went down so far that the bottom couldn't be seen. There was no sign of Jaime. The explorers knew the boy was in great danger.

Dr. Stewart was lowered on a long rope. Ten minutes later, three sharp tugs on the rope showed that he wanted to be raised.

"At the bottom, there's a fast-moving underground river," Dr. Stewart reported. "The river comes out of the ground onto some rocks. Jaime must be in the water somewhere. We have to find those rocks and follow the river."

(to be continued)

© Houghton Mifflin Harcourt Publishing Company

A **Circle the correct answer for each question.**

1. Why did Ethan not realize that the snake was on a branch?

   a. The snake's colors blended in with the colors of the tree.

   b. The snake was hidden in the hollow of a tree.

   c. The snake was completely in shadows.

   d. The snake had not made any noise.

2. Why did Jaime fall into the pit?

   a. He was busy photographing a bird.

   b. He wanted to see what was inside the pit.

   c. He tripped on a vine on the jungle floor.

   d. He was not watching where he was going.

3. What happened last in this part of the selection?

   a. The boa twisted around Ethan.

   b. Amanda arrived with help.

   c. Dr. Stewart located the pit.

   d. Jaime disappeared.

4. Read this sentence from the first paragraph.

   > Amanda and Rosa saw vibrant reds and yellows flashing through the jungle as a pair of birds flew from tree to vine.

   Which word in the first paragraph helps readers understand what *vibrant* means?

   a. bright

   b. shape

   c. study

   d. opportunity

5. Which words in the first three paragraphs signal an important change in tone?

   a. *an even more demanding job*

   b. *the girls gasped*

   c. *froze with fright*

   d. *creeping toward a thick tree trunk*

© Houghton Mifflin Harcourt Publishing Company

B **Answer the questions on the lines provided.**

1. Describe the reaction that Amanda and Rosa had right after Jaime fell down the pit and the boa squeezed itself even more tightly around Ethan. What does this tell you about the girls?

_____

_____

_____

_____

2. Describe how the rain forest changed from a pleasant place to a threatening place in this part of the selection.

_____

_____

_____

_____

3. Write a brief summary of this part of the selection.

_____

_____

_____

_____

© Houghton Mifflin Harcourt Publishing Company

Name _____ Date _____

 Almost every paragraph has two or more details that support a main idea. Read the following sentences and phrases. Label each one *Main Idea* or *Detail*.

Example:

_____Detail_____ a. high humidity

_____Detail_____ b. high temperatures

_____Detail_____ c. crowded trees and bushes

___Main Idea___ d. a rain forest or jungle

_____Detail_____ e. many noisy birds

_____Detail_____ f. many insects

_____Detail_____ g. brightly colored flowers

1.

_____ a. meat-eating plant

_____ b. long, slender buds

_____ c. pale, yellow color

_____ d. lovely flower when open

_____ e. eats insects

_____ f. has fragrance that attracts insects

2.

_____ a. The explorers brought in their supplies on burros.

_____ b. They brought food, tents, clothing, books, dishes, tools, and laptop computers.

_____ c. The explorers brought cameras, photographic supplies, and voice recorders.

_____ d. Everything that was necessary for life had to be brought into the jungle by the explorers.

_____ e. They brought medicine, medical supplies, and cleaning materials.

© Houghton Mifflin Harcourt Publishing Company

D **Read the paragraphs below. Underline the correct main idea for each.**

1. Plants and animals cannot exist without water. They must drink it. People need it for bathing, cooking, cleaning, growing crops, and for pleasure. Water helps spread seeds and is an important means of transportation for humans.

   a. Water is necessary for some living things.

   b. Water is necessary for all living things.

   c. Water makes possible transportation by boat.

2. Most lizards that live in forests are green or yellow. Those that live in deserts are dull red or brown. Jungle lizards are brightly colored.

   a. Lizards' coloring blends with the colors of the places where they live.

   b. Lizards are colorful so that they can attract mates.

   c. Jungle lizards do not have as many enemies as desert lizards.

3. The favorite food of mongooses is snakes. A mongoose almost always defeats a snake in battle. Mongooses attack by biting the back of the snake's neck. Sometimes a mongoose holds the snake's jaws shut so tightly that it is helpless. When the snake is too tired to fight, the mongoose eats it.

   a. Mongooses enjoy eating snakes, but they can seldom kill them.

   b. A snake can usually escape a mongoose by waiting until it is tired.

   c. Mongooses kill and eat snakes.

4. An emerald boa lies on a tree branch in a strange way. It seems to be tied in a fancy knot that is higher in the center. On the sides its body is in loops. The boa's head is found in the middle of the knot. When a victim approaches, the boa unties itself rapidly and strikes suddenly.

   a. The emerald boa lies with its head in the middle of a knot.

   b. The emerald boa's victims are monkeys, lizards, and birds.

   c. The emerald boa can surprise its victims by hiding on tree branches.

5. Crocodiles and alligators choose a dry, sunny spot close to the water for a nest. The mother makes a large pile of dirt, grass, and leaves. She lays eggs in the heap and covers them with more grass and mud. The mother guards the eggs by lying on them most of the time. She returns to the water only when searching for food. Other crocodiles lay their eggs in sand. The female digs a hole and deposits the eggs in the pit. The eggs are then covered well with more sand.

   a. Some crocodiles and alligators have nests in water or on land.

   b. The mother alligators and crocodiles seldom leave their nests unguarded.

   c. The nests of alligators and crocodiles are always built on land.

© Houghton Mifflin Harcourt Publishing Company

E The sentence that tells the main idea of a paragraph is called the topic sentence. The topic sentence can be found anywhere in the paragraph. Read the following paragraphs. Find the topic sentence and underline it in each paragraph.

1. What a struggle it was just to walk through the rain forest. There were no roads or paths through the thick trees and bushes. Weeds, sometimes covered with thorns, grew high. Twisted vines hung from trees like heavy curtains. The explorers had to cut or push their way through.

2. The explorers found several huge tarantulas in the forest. Tarantulas—very large, hairy spiders—are dangerous to man and beast. Their size allows them to attack birds and other small animals. Tarantulas bite victims. Even adult human beings can become ill from the bite of these spiders.

3. To be a fish, a creature must have fins, gills, and a backbone. A starfish has gills but no backbone or fins, so it is not really a fish. Since a whale has no gills, it is not a fish. A jellyfish has no fins, no gills, and no backbone. Is a jellyfish really a fish?

4. Most animals build their nests and homes in places where they will not be disturbed by enemies. It is also important that they protect their homes and families from nature. Strong winds, rain, and sun are troublesome to most animals. Furthermore, they usually live close to their food so they can eat and then retreat to their homes safely. In general, animals choose the location of their nests and homes carefully.

75

Selection 10

"Help!" screamed Jaime as his body continued its swift descent into the deep pit. His only thought was that he would be smashed on the bottom. The fall seemed to take forever!

Instead, he plunged into water! The water rushed along, turning him over and over. Jaime was a strong swimmer, but the current was so forceful that he was helpless.

He felt himself bump into rocks. It was too dark to see anything. Just as he realized that this river was under the ground, he was pushed out into bright sunlight. The force of water still carried him.

Jaime grabbed a rock, hung there, and looked around. He was shivering, and he knew it wasn't only because he was wet and cold. Just around the bend ahead, the rapids reached a sharp drop. The river went over the drop, forming a high waterfall.

The rapids tore at Jaime. He was about to lose his grip on the rock. His fear ballooned. Was he going to be swept over the waterfall?

Suddenly, the force of the current moved the rock! Jaime was tossed about like a bouncing ball. Overhead he saw a tree branch hanging over the rapids. If he could get closer to the side of the river, maybe he could grab the branch as he was swept by.

Only an excellent swimmer could fight against the strong current. Jaime never understood how he had managed to do it. But there he was at the riverbank.

© Houghton Mifflin Harcourt Publishing Company

Core Skills Reading Comprehension, Grade 6

He willed his tired arms to reach for the branch. For several minutes he hung there, trying to convince his muscles to act. At first they refused to cooperate.

Little by little, though, hand over hand, he worked his way along the branch. Finally, he was on land, completely exhausted and very thankful!

Meanwhile, the search party had found where the underground river flowed out into the rain forest. But the winding water was hard to follow through the thick vegetation. The group stopped frequently, beating through the bushes to see if Jaime had been washed up on the bank. The search took hours.

Jaime took a long rest on the riverbank. When he awoke, he smelled a fragrant perfume. Months of searching for the Mysteria had made it a habit for him to trace all odors. Like Boscoe, his bloodhound dog back home, he had to decide where the fragrance was strongest. He followed the scent as it became more powerful. It came from a dark cave in the rocks behind the waterfall.

Before going into the darkness. Jaime took off his torn shirt and ripped it into several pieces. He tied the pieces to trees to show the path he was taking in case his friends found his trail.

"I'm glad they made us wear bright orange shirts," he thought.

Jaime felt his way through the small cave, following the scent. At the far end, he saw light. Squeezing through a narrow crevice in the wall, he came out into a meadow. It was the first open space he had seen during his months-long stay in the rain forest.

What an unbelievable sight! Thousands of lovely Mysteria flowers stretched before his eyes. Each blossom had large, curly petals in shades of blue and purple. Jaime had never seen such beautiful flowers before. The fragrance was almost overpowering. "The perfume makers will be happy about this," thought Jaime.

Being a young scientist, he cautiously picked one flower and broke its stem. Inside he found an oily liquid that dripped out slowly. This was a possible cure for the disease!

Later, many of the flowers would be picked to take back to the United States. Seeds would be collected so that scientists could try to grow Mysterias in other countries. But, meanwhile, carrying a large bunch of fragrant Mysterias, Jimmy retraced his path to the riverbank. There he waited for the search party to find him.

© Houghton Mifflin Harcourt Publishing Company

A Circle the correct answer for each question.

1. Why did the explorers wear orange shirts?

   a. The color could be seen in river water.

   b. The color matched the flowers and bushes.

   c. The color stood out in the jungle.

   d. The color blended with the shadows.

2. Why did the author compare Jaime to a bloodhound?

   a. Jaime suddenly missed his dog.

   b. Jaime was panting.

   c. Jaime was following an odor.

   d. Jaime was wild and upset.

3. Why was it so difficult for Jaime to swim to the bank of the river?

   a. He was in a strong current.

   b. He found himself in an unfamiliar place.

   c. He had been injured when he fell into the pit.

   d. He was not a good swimmer.

4. What is this part of the selection mainly about?

   a. a waterfall, a cave, and a meadow

   b. a boy who could think for himself

   c. following a trail in the rain forest

   d. how to swim in rapids

5. Which of these best describes the tone of the last paragraph?

   a. emotional

   b. admiring

   c. lively

   d. practical

6. How will the search party *mostly likely* find Jaime?

   a. by swimming down the fast-flowing river

   b. by looking carefully on both sides of the river

   c. by going back to camp for a map of the rain forest

   d. by using bloodhound dogs to track him

© Houghton Mifflin Harcourt Publishing Company

B Answer the questions on the lines provided.

1. Why do you think the author included the paragraph about the search party in this part of the selection?

_____

_____

_____

2. Why would "Success by Accident" be a good title for this three-part selection?

_____

_____

_____

_____

C Write all the words from below that mean the same or almost the same as *a smell* or *to smell* or *to take in air*.

cents	sniff	stink
expect	odor	breathe
current	sent	swift
fragrance	inhale	descent
muscles	scent	aroma

1. _____   5. _____

2. _____   6. _____

3. _____   7. _____

4. _____   8. _____

© Houghton Mifflin Harcourt Publishing Company

Name _____ Date _____

D Find a word from below that is a synonym for the underlined word or words in each sentence. Then write each sentence using the new word.

swiftly	tossed	carefully
tracked	plunging	helpless

1. The swimmers were <u>diving</u> into the river.

   _____

2. The current of the river moved <u>quickly</u>.

   _____

3. Jaime <u>cautiously</u> broke the stem of the flower.

   _____

4. He was <u>thrown around</u> like a bouncing ball.

   _____

5. The bloodhound <u>followed the trail</u> of the lost camper.

   _____

E The main idea of a paragraph is usually told in the topic sentence. All the other sentences in the paragraph should give details or facts that support the topic sentence. Read these paragraphs. Underline the topic sentence of each paragraph. Then find one or more sentences in each paragraph that do not support the topic sentence. Draw a line through them.

Insects

1. Insects live in almost every kind of place. A few insects live in the sea, but most insects are found in fresh water or on land. Insects fly, crawl, hop, jump, walk, and swim. Insects live in the mountains, in deserts, in jungles, and in hot springs. Even in the ice and snow of the Antarctic, insects have been found. Insects can be different sizes and different colors.

2. All insects have two antennas, or feelers, on their heads. All have six legs and are covered with a waterproof material called chitin. There are more insects in the world than all other animals put together. The bodies of all insects are divided into three parts—the head, the abdomen, and the thorax. All insects have these things in common.

© Houghton Mifflin Harcourt Publishing Company

F Many times the title of a selection or a paragraph will give a clue about the main idea. Read each paragraph below and then choose the best title for it from the box. Write the title on the line above the paragraph.

Some Famous Waterfalls	Handle with Care
A Stubborn Animal	Kinds of Waterfalls
The Formation of Waterfalls	A Useful Animal

1. _____

Waterfalls are beautiful sights to see. Some are unbelievably lovely because the water drops for a very long distance. Others are lower but wider and have a huge curtain of water streaming down. A few, great waterfalls are both wide and high.

2. _____

A waterfall is a stream of water that drops freely over a cliff. It is formed when water flows over hard rocks first and then over softer ones. After thousands of years, the softer stones are worn down by the water. When the soft stones are gone, the water keeps on flowing, but over an empty space.

3. _____

Burros are a kind of donkey. Because they are strong and healthy, they can do a great deal of hard work. Neither heat nor freezing cold bothers them much. Unlike human beings, burros seldom seem to get sick. They can carry heavy loads for long distances, climb mountains, and cross deserts.

4. _____

Though burros are good workers, they cannot be trusted to work on their own. They are often tricky and want to do things their way. If an owner does not tie a burro when leaving it, the animal will just walk away and never return. The owner is left without transportation. The clever burro learns quickly what its owners want it to do. Then the burro tries in every way to do just the opposite.

81

G Some words have more than one meaning. Study the meanings of the two words. Read the sentences. Then decide which meaning fits each sentence. Write the correct letter of the meaning beside each sentence.

bank
    a. a place to save money
    b. rising ground bordering a body of water

current
    c. a movement of electricity
    d. in general use; generally accepted
    e. a flowing, onward motion; a stream, especially the fastest part of it

_____ **1.** The *current* swept the boat down the stream.

_____ **2.** The *current* style is to wear jeans.

_____ **3.** A hippo stood on the *bank* of the stream.

_____ **4.** She got a shock when the *current* came through the fallen wire.

_____ **5.** He put the money he earned in the *bank*.

_____ **6.** The crocodile walked down the *bank* and into the lake.

H Read the following paragraphs. Then answer the questions about the main ideas and the details.

cecropia Moth   **viceroy Butterfly**

  1.   Every part of the body of a moth or butterfly has a special purpose. The thorax is made up of three sections. One pair of legs is attached to each part. The front wings are attached to the middle part of the thorax. The rear wings are attached to the back section. Under the covering of the thorax are found the muscles that control the movement of the wings and legs.

© Houghton Mifflin Harcourt Publishing Company

2. The heads of moths and butterflies, like the heads of humans, have important uses. On the head are located the large eyes that stick out. They are compound eyes. That is, they are made up of many smaller sections to allow the insect to see in more than one direction at the same time. In this way, the insect can spot an enemy approaching from any direction. On the head are also found two antennae. They enable the butterfly or moth to smell and touch. The moth's antennae are feathery. The butterfly's antennae are like thin threads.

3. Color is more important to butterflies and moths than to any other animals. This is because butterflies and moths see colors. Cats, dogs, and some other animals see everything in shades of gray. Moths and butterflies see more colors than human beings. If flowers look lovely to you, they probably are more beautiful to a butterfly.

4. Besides seeing in color, moths and butterflies have bodies covered with color. This makes it easy for males and females of one kind to find each other. It helps them to spot a butterfly or moth of a different type moving in on their territory.

5. The colors on the wings are in spots, dots, and other patterns. In the air, these designs help conceal the insects from the sight of their enemies. The broken areas of color are even more important when the insects are resting. The colors provide protection. This allows the moths and butterflies to blend in with their surroundings. In this way, moths are different from butterflies. Moths rest with wings stretched out flat so that spots are found only on the tops of the wings. Butterflies rest with wings that are closed and held upright. Their bright color markings must be both on the top and bottom of the wings.

© Houghton Mifflin Harcourt Publishing Company

1. What is the main idea of paragraph 2? Write the topic sentence.

_____

_____

2. Which paragraph tells about the importance of the thorax? Circle the answer.

   a. paragraph 3   c. paragraph 4

   b. paragraph 2   d. paragraph 1

3. What is the main idea of paragraph 5? Circle the answer.

   a. Butterflies and moths see the colors of objects around them.

   b. Colors on the wings of butterflies and moths are formed in dots.

   c. Colors protect butterflies and moths while they are flying and resting.

   d. There are differences between butterflies and moths.

4. What does paragraph 3 mainly tell about?

   a. which colors butterflies can see best

   b. that butterflies blend with their surroundings

   c. that colors are seen by butterflies and moths

   d. that some animals do not see colors

5. Match the correct title with each paragraph. Write the letter for each title next to the correct paragraph number.

   _____ 1.   a. How Some Creatures See Colors

   _____ 2.   b. Colorful Protection

   _____ 3.   c. The Head and Its Parts

   _____ 4.   d. Bodies Covered with Color

   _____ 5.   e. What's on My Thorax?

6. If all five paragraphs were put together to form one selection, what would be the best title for the selection? Circle the answer.

   a. Spots, Dots, and Other Patterns

   b. Colorful Facts About Colorful Animals

   c. What Are You Picking Up on Your Antennae?

   d. Colorful Facts About Colorful Insects

© Houghton Mifflin Harcourt Publishing Company

Selection 11

Another Point of View

When Jaime stumbled into the meadow of Mysterias, he didn't know that he was being observed. The inhabitants living in and near the meadow concealed themselves noiselessly, but they watched the strange creature closely. They wondered whether it was a new enemy.

Among the inhabitants in the dense underbrush around the meadow was a colony of birds called gleaming dotted parakeets. The particular species of parakeet hadn't yet been discovered by humans. Their spots were of a variety of intense colors. No two birds had the same pattern or combination of colors. They had the usual parakeet shape and the small hooked beak, but their head was unusually large. And in this large head was a brain bigger than that of any other bird in the world.

These big-brained, intelligent birds could think clearly and quickly. They had learned to understand the languages of the other animals in the area. They didn't realize, because they had never seen a human before, that they would also be able to understand human languages. And—equally amazing—these clever birds could write!

Here are some pages from the diary of Cedric Parakeet. After you read them, answer the questions that follow.

September 5—For weeks I've had no thoughts to record in my diary because life has been dull. Our old enemies, the plaid owls, haven't even attacked us lately. We've enjoyed a huge crop of the seeds we love from all the blue and purple flowers around here. The yellow berries we enjoy are also in good supply. Lately, we parakeets have had nothing to do except open our beaks and let the food roll in.

Today, however, something exciting did happen. In the afternoon, a new creature stumbled into the meadow. It must be a bird because it walks on two legs as we do. It doesn't have wings, however, and it doesn't seem able to fly. When it first arrived, the creature rushed to the purple and blue flowers and sniffed them. Then it picked one. It broke the flower in half along the stem and carefully watched the sap oozing out. I've never seen a bird with so much curiosity.

© Houghton Mifflin Harcourt Publishing Company

September 6—I informed my mate, Zinnia, that I'm quite worried about the odd two-legged creature that is spending time in our meadow. "The bottom half of the creature has some strange covering," I told her. "It's certainly not feathers. Maybe it's fur. The top half of the creature is naked skin. The intense sunshine is making the creature's exposed skin turn red. How can I make it understand that it must crawl into the shadows?"

Zinnia flew to the edge of the meadow to look at the creature. When she returned, she announced, "I think it recently hatched from an egg. Just wait. Pinfeathers will soon grow out of its skin."

September 7—The two-legged creature must have realized the effects of the hot sun. Now it stays in the shade more. At times it goes through the cave to the rain forest. How strange that it remains there for hours. The rain forest is shadowy, gloomy, damp, and clammy.

I buzzed over the creature today and eyed its skin closely. No pinfeathers are growing yet. Later, when I told Zinnia, she said, "Speaking of feathers, you had better start building a new nest. We need it for the eggs I'm planning to sit on soon."

September 10—I had to neglect my diary for two days. Collecting feathers, strings, grass, and mud to build a parakeet nest is difficult work.

With all this flying about toting materials in my beak, I didn't have the energy to observe the two-legged creature. I did see it for a moment in the rain forest, sitting on the riverbank. It appears to be waiting for something to happen. I wonder if it found something good to eat in the mud there. Maybe it eats insects and worms.

September 11—Today the two-legged featherless bird saw me for the first time. I was admiring the nest I had built. Zinnia has been sitting on three tiny eggs since yesterday. I was busy bringing her some delicious yellow berries to eat. I'll confess that in my haste I was a bit careless. The creature must have seen me carrying berries into the tangle of vines. The first thing Zinna and I knew, a gigantic flipper roughly pushed back the vine leaves, and then a tremendous face hung over our nest. The size of that face seemed threatening. I could see plainly that there were no pinfeathers sprouting on that face yet. But the head did have some thin black strings growing on the top and down the sides.

"It's all your fault, Cedric!" screeched Zinnia. "The creature followed you and found us. And now it's going to eat us!"

My wings quivered with fright. This was surely the end for Zinnia, the eggs, and me!

Then the tremendous mouth opened and words came out—words that Zinnia and I could understand! How could that be? We had never heard this creature's language before, and yet we understood it!

© Houghton Mifflin Harcourt Publishing Company

"Wow!" said the strange bird. "What beautiful parakeets these are, covered with spots of brilliant colors. They're more amazing than any of the butterflies or flowers I've seen in the rain forest. I wish I had my camera. When the search party comes, they'll want to photograph this unusual sight."

"What's a camera?" I chirped. "What does *photograph* mean?"

At that moment I realized that, even though we could understand most of what the creature said, it couldn't understand us. What a disappointment.

September 12—Zinnia is still sitting on the eggs. The strange animal still has no pinfeathers. It hangs around Zinnia and me when it isn't in the rain forest. Mostly it sits or lies down and stuffs its mouth with berries and bananas.

Zinnia and I get nervous when it stands in the underbrush. It's a little disturbing to see those tremendous brown eyes suddenly peering into our nest.

"How are the babies?" it inquires politely each time. "Are they pecking their way out of the eggs yet?"

Zinnia always replies, even though the creature can't understand, "They're not ready to hatch. It takes three weeks for them to emerge."

The creature loves to talk to us. The words pour out. Its pink tongue flaps and flaps.

"I got here on September 5, and today is September 12. That means I've been here one whole week," it complained to us. "Will the search party ever find me?"

By now the creature has realized that we understand his language. We answered by nodding our heads yes.

© Houghton Mifflin Harcourt Publishing Company

September 13—The creature asked Zinnia and me to go away with it when the search party arrives. We didn't nod our heads this time.

It turns out that our large featherless friend has its uses. Earlier today, it puts its huge flipper over the nest and kept the eggs warm so Zinnia and I could leave to visit relatives.

September 15—We now love our overgrown bird friend! Yesterday the plaid owls arrived, mean and hungry. One had already grabbed an older parakeet in its talons when our strange creature intervened. It used a broken branch to beat off the enormous plaid owl. Then, when the enemy owl's talons opened, our featherless friend caught the old parakeet as it fell to the ground.

Now Zinnia and I can't even get near the creature! All our friends and relatives stay perched on its head, flippers, and shoulders, showing our gratitude.

September 16—It happened today! The search party arrived! They had similar, but slightly different features from those of our bird friend. First they hugged our creature and screamed, "Jaime!" (What's a *Jaime*?) Then they ran through the field of blue and purple flowers, inhaling their fragrance and smiling. After that they started breaking flower stems.

September 17—The creature, Jaime, showed us off to the search party. We were all there, except Zinnia of course. She was still sitting on the eggs.

"I can tell that the parakeets understand every word we say," announced Jaime to the other members of the search party.

"They must come home with us!" exclaimed one of them. "During all my exploration, they're the most fascinating birds I've ever seen!"

"They're the most intelligent, too," Jaime added.

September 18—Today we found out what a camera is—also what *photography* means. All morning the new creatures took pictures of Zinnia on the nest. They even gently lifted her to take a close-up picture of the eggs.

September 19—Some of the parakeets have decided to go home with the humans, as the creatures are called. Zinnia and I won't. We're still waiting for the eggs to hatch.

© Houghton Mifflin Harcourt Publishing Company

September 20—There I was, all alone on the nest. All the other parakeets had flown to the rain forest, either to chirp farewell to the humans or to leave with them. Then I heard that old, familiar crashing through the underbrush. I knew it had to be clumsy Jaime.

And I was right. He came up to the nest and said, "My family and I will wait until your babies have hatched. You were so good to me, and I want to give you a safe home in return."

Zinnia and I have always loved adventure. And the idea of living in a safe place is attractive. So we've decided to accept Jaime's offer. Soon we'll be saying good-bye to our meadow.

A Circle the correct answer for each question.

1. What could Jaime *not* do?

   a. eat the berries growing near the meadow

   b. understand the parakeets' language

   c. protect the parakeets from an enemy

   d. talk to the parakeets

2. Why did Cedric's friends and relatives come to love Jaime?

   a. Jaime invited all of them to go back home with him.

   b. Jaime brought them food.

   c. Jaime could understand what they were saying.

   d. Jaime rescued them from danger.

3. Which sentence from the selection is a clue to something that happens later in the selection?

   a. *Our old enemies, the plaid owls, haven't even attacked us lately.*

   b. *Lately, we parakeets have had nothing to do except open our beaks and let the food roll in.*

   c. *Zinnia flew to the edge of the meadow to look at the creature. When she returned, she announced, "I think it recently hatched from an egg."*

   d. *The two-legged creature must have realized the effects of the hot sun. Now it stays in the shade more.*

4. Which of the following should *not* go in a summary of Cedric's diary entries?

   a. A two-legged creature arrives in the meadow.

   b. The parakeets have a good supply of yellow berries to eat.

   c. Cedric builds a nest in which Zinnia's eggs will hatch.

   d. When the plaid owls attack the parakeets, the two-legged creature fights them off.

© Houghton Mifflin Harcourt Publishing Company

5. What does the title of the selection, "Another Point of View," mean?

    a. The world looks different to a creature living in a meadow than it does to a creature living in a rain forest.

    b. The parakeets watch everything the humans do so they can become more intelligent than them.

    c. Jaime and the explorers appear very different to the parakeets than they do to other humans.

    d. Jaime changes his opinion of parakeets after he has spent a few weeks with them.

B   **Answer the questions on the lines provided.**

1. Describe how the tone changes in the first paragraph of the diary entry for September 11. Name specific word choices that the author made.

_____

_____

_____

2. For Cedric, the rain forest is "shadowy, gloomy, damp, and clammy," and he cannot understand why Jaime spends time there. Explain what the rain forest is for Jaime.

_____

_____

3. Cedric sees Jaime in one way. Jaime sees himself in a very different way. Complete the chart to compare their different viewpoints.

What Jaime sees	What Cedric sees
a. _____	two-legged featherless creature
b. _____	strange covering that isn't feathers
c. _____	flipper
d. _____	black strings

© Houghton Mifflin Harcourt Publishing Company

C **Think, skim the selection and diary entries, and use a calendar to answer these questions.**

1. How many days are in September?

   _____

2. Which month comes just before September?

   _____

3. How many days was Jimmy in the meadow before the search party found him?

   _____

4. How many weeks was that?

   _____

5. How many days does it take for parakeet eggs to hatch?

   _____

6. Around what date will baby birds emerge from Zinnia's eggs?

   _____

7. When did Jimmy chase away plaid owls?

   _____

8. In which month were the Mysterias finally discovered?

   _____

91

© Houghton Mifflin Harcourt Publishing Company

D **Write a word from below to complete each sentence.**

haste	conceal	gleaming	dense
apologize	exhausted	talons	intervene
clammy	toting	neglect	quiver

1. Another word for *carrying* is _____.

2. To fail to do one's duty or work is to _____ it.

3. To say, "I'm sorry," is to _____.

4. Something that is damp and chilly is _____.

5. Something that is reflecting light is _____.

6. To make oneself difficult to see is to _____.

7. To interfere with the outcome of something is to _____.

8. Claws of some birds are _____.

9. Underbrush that is growing thickly is described as _____.

10. To flutter or shake slightly is to _____.

11. Quickness that can cause a mistake is _____.

© Houghton Mifflin Harcourt Publishing Company

Selection 12

This is a myth from the Asian country of Thailand.

In the water that laps the shores of Thailand, there once lived a sea princess named Maykala (Mā′ kǎ′ lə). Her father, king of the sea, loved her dearly. Maykala was beautiful and fun-loving. She liked to swim in the waves and tease the fish. Only when dark clouds covered the sky did she stop having fun and dive down to her father's castle.

One day the king of the sea called to Maykala and said, "Maykala, it is time for you to marry. I have chosen the great Lord Siva (Sǐ′ va) to be your husband."

This made the sea princess unhappy. She wanted to splash in the cool blue-green water and swim with the silver fish. She liked the sunshine, which made her flash like crystal on the waves. But to please her father, Maykala agreed to marry Lord Siva.

Just before the wedding, the sea king gave his daughter a beautiful present. It was a crystal ball.

He said, "When you feel sad or lonely, polish the crystal ball. Then look into it, and you will remember your home and the good times you had with your friends."

Lord Siva married the sea princess and took her to his palace in the sky. With time, Maykala came to love the palace. Since it was her nature to enjoy herself, she made many friends.

© Houghton Mifflin Harcourt Publishing Company

One day she wandered through the airy palace. She realized that all the other gods had left to do their work. Only the guards, whose duty it was to watch over her and protect her, were there. A feeling of loneliness swept over her.

She said to herself, "Oh! I wish I could go outside the sky palace! If I could only go past the gates, then I could play in the sun."

Maykala remembered her father's gift. She found the crystal ball and began to polish it. When she looked into it, she could recall the beautiful sea that had once been her home. The silver waves dazzled her eyes in the brilliant sunshine. She decided to take the crystal ball outside to collect all the colors of the rainbow in it. Then she would have memories of her present home reflected in the ball.

Quietly, Maykala crept on tiptoe to the gate. She saw that the guards were asleep, so she rushed past them. Suddenly overcome by a desire to dance, she skipped from one soft cloud to the next. As she danced, she let the crystal ball absorb the colors of the rainbow. She felt happy and free in the warm air.

Then, Maykala became aware of a large shadow covering her. She looked up and saw an evil-looking giant glaring down at her. Dark rain clouds hung to his black cape.

"What are you doing here? Who are you, girl?" he snarled in anger.

Maykala was scared at first. Then she thought that since she was the wife of the great Lord Siva, this evil-looking giant had no right to talk to her in such a tone of voice. She said, "Who are *you* to talk to me that way?"

This made the giant even more irate. He roared so loudly that he caused the clouds to shake and the wind to blow. Down on the earth, huge trees fell, and gigantic waves rose up on the seas.

The giant roared, "I am Ramasoon (Rǎ´ mǎ sūn). No one dares to talk to *me* like that."

Maykala quickly skipped to another cloud. With his black cape that held dark rain clouds fluttering around him, Ramasoon raised his large ax to throw at the princess.

Maykala quickly pointed the crystal ball at the sun. The dazzling light from the sun reflected off the ball and flashed into the giant's eyes, momentarily blinding him. With a deep roar, he threw his ax. It missed the princess and fell to the earth with a crash. Maykala laughed at the giant, which made him even angrier. While he went down to the earth to pick up his ax, Maykala quickly skipped to another cloud and waited for the giant's return.

© Houghton Mifflin Harcourt Publishing Company

Once again Ramasoon yelled and threw his ax, and once again Maykala flashed the crystal ball in his eyes. This time, when the ax missed its target, Ramasoon bellowed and let his black cape fly out behind him to free the dark clouds there. Then the rain poured down to the earth.

Maykala decided to stop playing games. She had had enough fun for one day. She returned to the palace and tiptoed softly into her room. She dried her hair and then rotated her crystal ball so she could see all the colors of the rainbow glittering inside.

So once a year, every year, all the gods in Lord Siva's palace leave to do their work. Maykala becomes lonely and wanders through the empty rooms. She escapes past the guards and plays hide-and-seek with Ramasoon, the ugly giant. Every time she flashes her crystal ball in his eyes, he throws his ax at her and misses. When the ax falls to the earth, Thailand's rainy season begins, and heavy storms lash the country.

The children of Thailand are never afraid of thunder and lightning. They know what is happening when they see lightning streak through the sky and hear the loud crash of thunder. Ramasoon, the ugly giant, is pursuing Maykala, the lonely sea princess, across the heavens. And they know he will never catch her.

© Houghton Mifflin Harcourt Publishing Company

A Circle the correct answer for each question.

1. Where did *most* of the selection take place?

   a. inside Lord Siva's palace

   b. inside the castle of Maykala's father

   c. in the heavens

   d. in the ocean

2. Which of these *best* describes Maykala?

   a. She could tell the future by looking at her crystal ball.

   b. She was the goddess of all sea creatures.

   c. She could cause the clouds to shake and the winds to blow.

   d. She was a playful sea goddess.

3. When did Ramasoon throw his ax at Maykala?

   a. before Maykala flashed her crystal ball at Ramasoon

   b. after Maykala flashed her crystal ball at Ramasoon

   c. at the same time that Maykala flashed her crystal ball at Ramasoon

   d. after Maykala showed Ramasoon her crystal ball

4. What power did Ramasoon have?

   a. He could push all the colors of the rainbow into a crystal ball.

   b. He could create heavy rains and terrible storms.

   c. He could make the sea princess do as he wished.

   d. He could make the sun move in the heavens.

5. Read this sentence from the selection. It occurs at the point in the selection when Maykala sees Ramasoon for the first time.

   > This made the giant even more irate.

   Which phrase from the selection *best* helps readers understand what *irate* means?

   a. *Down on the earth*

   b. *wife of the great Lord Siva*

   c. *snarled in anger*

   d. *so loudly*

© Houghton Mifflin Harcourt Publishing Company

Name _____ Date _____

B **Answer the questions on the lines provided.**

1. What was the greatest difference between Maykala and Ramasoon?

_____

_____

_____

2. Name the event in the myth that explains each of the following: lightning, thunder, heavy rain.

_____

_____

_____

_____

C **Circle the two antonyms in each group of words below.**

1. roar	recall	collect	forget
2. polishing	glaring	smiling	protecting
3. gigantic	tiny	unhappy	evil
4. serious	dazzling	beautiful	fun-loving
5. catch	bellow	pursue	tiptoe
6. choose	insult	scatter	collect
7. brilliantly	momentarily	permanently	mightily

© Houghton Mifflin Harcourt Publishing Company

D People that lived a long time ago made up myths to try to explain things they could not understand. They decided superhuman gods and goddesses caused and controlled events of nature and everyday life. Here are some characters from myths of different lands. What facts of nature were early people trying to explain? Write the fact under the myth.

> what rainbows were
>
> how sunshine on the waves made them glitter
>
> what the stars were
> what happened when winter came
>
> how day and night came about
>
> what thunder was

1. In Roman myths, Pluto, the king of the underworld, stole the lovely daughter of the harvest goddess. The world became cold and snowy. No crops could grow. What did this myth try to explain?

_____

2. In the Thai myth, Maykala was the daughter of the sea god. The ocean was her playground. As she danced and ran on the rippling waves, she flashed like crystal on top of the water. What did this myth try to explain?

_____

3. Helios was the god of the sun. Every day he drove his chariot across the sky, giving the world light. When he reached the end, he disappeared. However, he returned again each day at dawn to drive his chariot through the heavens. What did this myth try to explain?

_____

© Houghton Mifflin Harcourt Publishing Company

Name _____ Date _____

E **Match the correct effect to its cause. Write the letter of the effect beside its cause.**

CAUSE	EFFECT

_____ **1.** Because Maykala used to live in the water,

a. winds blew and waves arose on the seas.

_____ **2.** Because the guards were sleeping,

b. she skipped from cloud to cloud.

_____ **3.** Because Maykala was the wife of Lord Shiva,

c. they are not afraid of thunder and lightning.

_____ **4.** Because Maykala's father was afraid she would be lonely,

d. she was called the sea princess.

_____ **5.** Because Ramasoon roared,

e. Ramasoon was blinded for a short time.

_____ **6.** Because Maykala wanted to dance,

f. she married Lord Siva.

_____ **7.** Because Maykala pointed the crystal ball at the sun,

g. Maykala was able to sneak out of Lord Siva's palace.

_____ **8.** Because Maykala wanted to please her father,

h. she left her home in the sea.

_____ **9.** Because Maykala married Lord Siva,

i. he gave her a crystal ball.

_____ **10.** Because the children of Thailand know the myth of Maykala and Ramasoon,

j. she questioned Ramasoon's right to speak rudely to her.

99

© Houghton Mifflin Harcourt Publishing Company

Name _____   Date _____

Selection 13

Joseph Coburn, 28, was a photographer working for *Daring Adventures Magazine.* One Friday the thirteenth, his assignment was to cover a skydiving event.

"I never realized how superstitious I was until that day. I didn't even want to get out of bed!" Coburn has since claimed. "I knew this was Adam North's thirteenth jump, and it was happening on Friday the thirteenth. I was trembling from fright when I packed my gear and drove to the airport."

Coburn was to photograph the stunt divers from the local skydiving club. He and a pilot, Tracy Ortiz, planned to photograph the jumpers from the time they leaped from the plane until they landed safely on the field below.

Ortiz, 43, brought the plane close enough for Coburn to follow the jumps of Lou Girard, Agnes Brent, Liz Fratelli, and Ravi Sharma. They successfully completed some difficult stunts before opening their parachutes. Coburn was able to take some color photographs from unusual angles. They are so clear that one can even see the different facial expressions of the jumpers as they fell.

Then came Adam North, 23, making his thirteenth dive. He had been skydiving for five years. In a moment of carelessness, North forgot to keep his body in the jumper's arch—legs, arms, and head back—as he leaped. Joseph Coburn realized what was happening and kept taking photos as he followed the drama in the sky. On film, he caught North as he tried to open the parachute while tumbling the 3,600 feet toward the ground. The parachute's lines became tangled around North's legs. Next, the parachute wrapped around him like a plastic bag. From waist to toe, North was covered by folds of nylon fabric. Coburn's camera kept on clicking.

© Houghton Mifflin Harcourt Publishing Company

"The other chute!" Tracy Ortiz was yelling over and over. North opened his reserve parachute. It, too, twisted around the skydiver. Joseph Coburn groaned as the camera recorded the agony on Adam North's face.

By this time, North was falling at a great speed. He stayed calm, however, and tried to relax his body. Ortiz and Coburn shook their heads in pity. They were sure North was "a goner."

The camera recorded the stuntman rapidly falling toward a river. Now it was too dangerous for the photographer and the pilot to follow closely. But they did get a shot of North's plunge into the water, which was deep after two weeks of rain. People on the riverbank were able to pull North out. Coburn and Ortiz saw those people jumping up and down in apparent joy. At that moment they realized that the skydiver was alive.

An ambulance took North to the hospital. He had a broken leg and rib and bruised kidneys, but, considering the height he had fallen from, he was in good shape. The photographer and the pilot won several awards for excellent reporting and photography. Adam North's award was the fact that he had survived such a fall.

This event captured the interest of many people. It was described in a book, a television show, and several magazine articles. It was also made into a movie. In all of these versions, facts were supposedly told the way they had happened. However, some of the versions included extra parts that were not true and had been added. Selections with made-up parts are called *fiction*.

In some cases you will be told that a selection is true when it is really fiction. You must check all the facts yourself. Then you will be able to tell whether the selection that you are reading is *fact* or *fiction*.

© Houghton Mifflin Harcourt Publishing Company

A You have read the selection about Adam North. You know what is true. Now read about him in some other sources. Label each one *fiction* or *fact*.

_____ **1.** A movie called *The World Turned Upside Down*:

The director says, "This exciting adventure film tells the story of brave Joseph Coburn and Tracy Ortiz, a photographer and a pilot, who are taking pictures from a plane of skydivers doing stunts. When a skydiver becomes tangled in his parachute, the clever pilot radios the airport for help. At the same time, he brings the airplane under the falling man. Coburn and Ortiz manage to catch the falling skydiver, thus carrying out the first midair rescue of a person! This film should pack in the audiences."

_____ **2.** A book called *Free Falls*:

The publishing company announced, "This is a book of photographs taken over two years by Joseph Coburn. They are studies of the training and the work of skydivers. He shows every step in the teaching and practicing of this exciting and popular sport. The text accompanying these prizewinning photos was written by Tracy Luis Ortiz, the pilot who has worked with Coburn in his study of skydivers. Ortiz, besides being a brave and skillful flier, writes clearly and beautifully. His reports make the reader live through the hopes, fears, joys, and sorrows of skydivers.

"The book includes pictures of the thrilling fall of Adam North, whose parachute failed to work. Ortiz, a friend of North, describes his own feelings as he watched his pal drop toward what he thought would be North's certain death."

© Houghton Mifflin Harcourt Publishing Company

Name _____ Date _____

_____ **3.** A magazine article called *Great Escapes*:

This article tells the stories of nine people who narrowly escaped being killed in accidents. Among the nine is Adam North, who lived to tell the tale after he plunged to the earth when both of his parachutes failed to open. With fascinating details, he describes how he felt during his fall, his rescue, and his recovery from the injuries he sustained.

_____ **4.** A television show called *The Sky's the Limit*:

On this program, skydiving and free-falling were described and photographed. The reporters visited several skydiving clubs and schools. They spoke to many teachers and students.

The photographers took pictures as a reporter interviewed Adam North, Tracy Ortiz, and Joseph Coburn about North's famous fall into a river after his two parachutes twisted around his body instead of floating him safely to the ground.

It was on this program that North first announced to the world that he would no longer be skydiving. The leg he had injured when he plunged into the river had not healed well. His doctors felt that the leg could no longer bear the strain of parachute landings.

103

© Houghton Mifflin Harcourt Publishing Company

Selection 13
Core Skills Reading Comprehension, Grade 6

B **Circle the correct answer for each question.**

1. What was Joseph Coburn's profession?

   a. stunt skydiver

   b. pilot

   c. ambulance driver

   d. photographer

2. How old was Adam North when he started skydiving?

   a. 15

   b. 18

   c. 23

   d. 28

3. Which of these events happened first?

   a. The parachute twisted around North's body.

   b. Ortiz, the pilot, yelled instructions to North.

   c. North forgot to keep his body in the jumper's arch.

   d. North tried to open his main parachute.

4. Which of the following from the selection *best* shows how North was feeling during his fall?

   a. *From waist to toe, North was covered by folds of nylon fabric.*

   b. *Joseph Coburn groaned as the camera recorded the agony on Adam North's face.*

   c. *By this time, North was falling at a great speed.*

   d. *Ortiz and Coburn shook their heads with pity. They were sure North was "a goner."*

5. Which of these should *not* be included in a summary of the selection?

   a. Four skydivers completed some difficult stunts before it was Adam North's turn.

   b. Joseph Coburn was assigned to photograph skydivers jumping from a plane.

   c. When Adam North jumped from the plane, he forgot to keep his body in the jumper's arch.

   d. Adam North survived falling from the plane, but he did have some injuries.

6. Which of these best describes the organization of the information in the selection?

   a. A problem and its solution are described.

   b. Careful skydivers are compared to a careless skydiver.

   c. Events are told in the order in which they happened.

   d. An opinion of the author is supported by several facts.

© Houghton Mifflin Harcourt Publishing Company

Name _____ Date _____

C **Answer the questions on the lines provided.**

1. How is Joseph Coburn introduced to the reader?

_____

_____

_____

2. How does the illustration on the first page of the selection help you as a reader?

_____

_____

_____

© Houghton Mifflin Harcourt Publishing Company

Many advertisements try to convince you to buy certain products, even if you do not need them or if they are not as good as other products. As the buyer, should be aware of the persuasive techniques used in advertisements. Persuasive advertisements may not give much reliable information about the product being sold. Instead, they may use persuasive techniques, or ways, to convince you to buy the product.

PERSUASIVE TECHNIQUES OF SELLING

1. Some ads tell you that famous actors, singers, athletes, or rich people buy and use the product.

2. Some ads tell you that everyone else is buying the product and that you should buy it, too, to be one of "the crowd."

3. Some ads tell you that there is a new, secret ingredient in the product that makes it better than any other company's.

D Here are some newspaper, Internet, and television ads. Read each one. Put a ✔ beside each ad that gives you the information you need to know about a product. If the ad tries to persuade you through a persuasive technique, write the number of the type of technique that is in the box above.

_____ 1.

Excitement and fun at home!
Enjoy hundreds of games!
Sports! Space monsters! Mazes!
Only $48.27.
Strong, well-made controls.
On-screen directions. Easy to operate.
One-year guarantee. Your money back
if not satisfied.

_____ 2. Six out of ten doctors recommend the
Frizzee Curling Iron. It's safe for any
type of hair. Bonnie and Johnnie,
famous singers, say, "Frizzee helped
to make us what we are today."

106

_____ 3.

Are these snowy days giving you sore, red, chapped hands? Cheer up! Help is on the way! Eppiss Company is having a sale on all their gloves. Warm leather gloves and mittens with silk, fur, or dacron linings reduced from $22.88 to $12.95. Beautiful wool gloves, fully lined, reduced from $9.98 to $6.50. Sold at all fine stores.

_____ 4.

At last, the mystery of the Sphinx is told! From the mummies comes the secret of the ingredient that made Cleopatra so slim and beautiful— *Glexo-Vitaheva-Dorpokeloline.* Only *Slinky* contains this magic ingredient that kills the extra calories you eat each day. Just eat, then take a *Slinky.* Everything else you eat for four hours doesn't count! After all, have you ever seen a fat mummy?

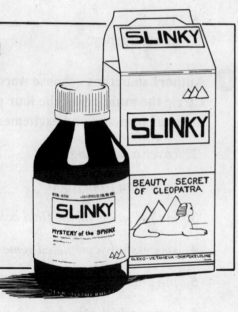

_____ 5.

Don't make your kids feel left out. And "left out" is what they'll feel without Zedoz Hyena shirts. Kids around the world are wearing these famous shirts. In Europe, Australia, New Zealand, Japan, North America, and South America, 9 out of 10 kids proudly display a hyena over their heart.

© Houghton Mifflin Harcourt Publishing Company

E Choose a word to complete each sentence.

bear	drama	gear	stunt
reserve	survivors	description	superstitious

1 Those not killed in an accident are called _____.

2. A _____ person feels uncomfortable on Friday the thirteenth.

3. The photographer's _____ took up too much room in the car.

4. North's leg could no longer _____ the strain of parachute landings.

5. One skydiver performed a _____ that was extremely dangerous.

6. The _____ parachute was extra and would be used only in case of an emergency.

F Authors sometimes choose words carefully to create a certain mood in their writing. Circle the numbers of the four phrases from the selection that *best* help to create a mood of suspense and excitement.

1. *cover a skydiving event*

2. *trembling from fright*

3. *landed safely on the field below*

4. *successfully completed some difficult stunts*

5. *the drama in the sky*

6. *water, which was deep*

7. *the agony on Adam North's face*

8. *Ortiz and Coburn shook their heads in pity*

© Houghton Mifflin Harcourt Publishing Company

Factual material can be proven true. The details can be checked in records or in the words of eyewitnesses.

Fictional material can be based on facts. However, the author of fictional material might do some of the things listed in the box below. If any of these are present in shows, movies, plays, or writings, they are fictional materials.

> **Fiction:**
>
> - includes details that cannot possibly fit the time period.
>
> - includes impossible actions, events, or deeds.
>
> - makes up characters that did not exist but that act, talk, and dress as if they could have existed.
>
> - contains characters such as ogres, giants, elves, witches, plants, animals, and people that are unheard of in real life.

G **Here are some parts of selections. These authors did not intend to write fiction. Some of the authors, however, changed factual material into fictional material based on fact. Label each selection *fiction* or *fact*.**

_____ 1. One of the most important dates in American history is July 4, 1776. On that date, the 13 colonies adopted the Declaration of Independence. The colonies at that time were ruled by England. For some time, one colonial group or another had wanted to gain freedom from England, but each group was too weak to break free alone.

_____ 2. Only when the 13 colonies banded together did they have enough strength to challenge the British king. The colonists formed the Continental Congress, with representatives from each colony. These representatives met for almost a year to decide what course of action to take.

109

3.   After a year's work, the Continental Congress decided what to do. They wrote a declaration of why the colonies wanted their freedom. They told of unfair acts of England against them. They declared that no longer would they remain colonies. Instead, all 13 colonies would form an independent country.

Thomas Jefferson wrote most of the Declaration of Independence. The ideas, however, were the result of work by him and others, such as Benjamin Franklin, Martin Luther King, Jr., and John Hancock.

4.   "Listen!" exclaimed Cyrus Lee. "The Liberty Bell is ringing!"

Cyrus, a thirteen-year-old cobbler's son, lived in Philadelphia in 1876.

"Hurry!" shouted his sister, Lizzie, running to the door of the small shop. "We will miss the reading of the Declaration of Independence!"

The bell was calling everyone in town to come to the square to hear what their leaders had decided to do. Before joining the crowd, however, Cyrus and Lizzie had to lock the door of their father's shop.

5.   In Washington, DC, you can see the Declaration of Independence. Some of the patriots scribbled when they signed their names. Their writing is barely legible. Others wrote very clearly. But John Hancock's signature is the largest and clearest on it.

© Houghton Mifflin Harcourt Publishing Company

_____ **6.** John Hancock's mother always punished him when his handwriting was sloppy. Many times he had to practice for two hours after school, writing with black and red markers in his loose-leaf notebook. Mrs. Hancock didn't realize that her efforts would make her son's signature the most outstanding one on the Declaration of Independence.

_____ **7.** The Declaration was signed by 56 men, representing the 13 colonies. John Hancock was the president of the Continental Congress at the time. He and the other brave men signing the document knew that this act would probably bring a war. They risked their lives, their homes, and their fortunes.

H If you wish to find information about John Hancock's school days at Boston Latin School, you can look in many places. Some of these writings below from books, stories, and articles are relevant, which means they are likely to contain facts on that topic. Others are not relevant. They would not give information about Hancock's education.

Write *relevant* in front of the four references that are *most likely* to contain true and relevant material about Hancock's education. Underline all the material in the others that would make it *not* relevant to Hancock's education. The first one has been done for you.

_____ **1.** *Child's Day Magazine* published an article called "William Deering at Boston Latin School." It is the true story of a man who was a pupil at the famous school in the years 1904 to 1910.

_____ **2.** John Adams kept a diary while he was a pupil at Boston Latin School at about the same time as John Hancock. The boys knew each other well. Both grew up to be signers of the Declaration of Independence. In his diary, the young John Adams wrote some complaints about his school days. One time his schoolmaster gave him a sound beating.

© Houghton Mifflin Harcourt Publishing Company

_____ 3. A set of encyclopedias contains in Volume 4 a long
article describing the everyday lives of people in the
Massachusetts, Virginia, Maryland, and South Carolina
colonies from 1700 to 1775.

_____ 4. A book entitled *United States History from 1850 to
1980* was published in 1982.

_____ 5. A book called *The Lives of Infants and Children in
English Colonies in America* was written by Mabel Sterling
Davis in 1804. She was born in New York in 1774. Some
of her family fought in the Revolutionary War.

_____ 6. *Learning Can Be Fun Magazine* includes three stories in
each issue which tell exciting adventures about history. In
the November issue are these three stories: "A Schoolboy
of Old Wyoming"; "Beulah, a Girl of Colonial Georgia";
and "Fiona and Angus of Virginia."

_____ 7. A book called *Education in the American Colonies*
gives an outline of how children were taught in British
colonies before they gained their independence. Famous
colonial schools in Boston, Charleston, and Richmond
are described.

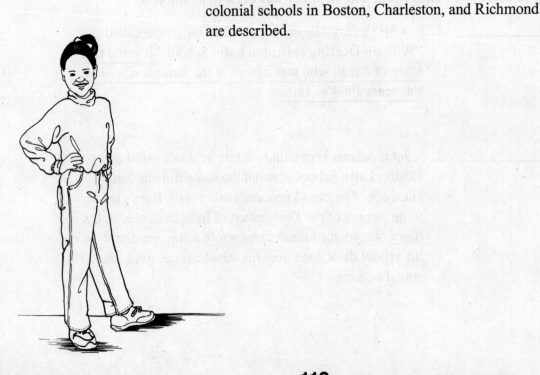

© Houghton Mifflin Harcourt Publishing Company

Skills Review: Selections 8–13

A Circle the two antonyms in each group of words below.

1. dangerous   trembling   brave   still

2. heal   injure   plunge   escape

3. narrator   survivor   witness   victim

4. toss   push   grab   release

B Circle the two synonyms in each group of words below.

1. sturdy   stuck   stable   stolen

2. protest   convince   persuade   attract

3. force   flutter   rotate   spin

4. glittering   dazzling   reflecting   glaring

C Read the selection below. Note the details. Underline the topic sentence or main idea in each paragraph. Then answer the questions.

If a sunflower is in a garden with many other kinds of flowers, it will be the first one noticed. That is because it is very tall, sometimes reaching ten or fifteen feet. Each long stem is topped by a huge flower.

The sunflower head, which is shaped like a very large daisy, is colorful. The petals are usually yellow. They are around a center, which can be black, brown, yellow, or purple.

In the morning, when the sun rises in the east, sunflowers face in that direction. At noon they raise their head to the sun directly above them. When the sun sets in the west, the flowers are facing west. Sunflowers always face the light.

Many birds eat sunflower seeds. In some countries, the seeds are pressed to get out the oil. The oil is used in making salad oil and margarine. The mashed seed left after the pressing is used to feed livestock such as cows and sheep. It is clear that sunflower seeds are very useful.

1. What is paragraph 2 mainly about?

    a. the petals of the sunflower

    b. the stem of the sunflower

    c. the appearance of sunflowers

    d. the uses of sunflowers

© Houghton Mifflin Harcourt Publishing Company

2. What is paragraph 3 mainly about?

_____

_____

3. In which paragraph should the following detail go?

> American scientists have been experimenting with using sunflower oil to run tractors.

_____

_____

4. What is the best title for the selection?

a. A Useful Giant

b. The Tallest Flower

c. Sunflowers for Farm Animals

d. Facing the Sun

© Houghton Mifflin Harcourt Publishing Company

D Here are two young researchers looking for information for reports. They each have a different topic. Look at the pictures to see what they are researching. Read the titles of the books that may help. Write the names of the relevant books next to each picture.

---

a. *The Hook and Ladder Trucks*

b. *The Know Everything Encyclopedia, Vol. 2 Ba–Ce*

c. *Night Watchmen of 1700 to 1840*

d. *Modern Russian Coins 1917–1992*

e. *The Know-Everything Encyclopedia, Vol. 7 Lu–My*

f. *Early Fire Prevention Measures 1680–1900*

g. *French Currency Since 1789*

h. *U.S. Sheriffs Until 1895*

i. *English Coins 1800–1914*

j. *The Fire Department Joke Book*

k. *Crime in the U.S. 1776–1886*

l. *History of Italian Coins*

1.

My topic is "European Money in the 1800s."

1. _____

2. _____

3. _____

4. _____

2.

My topic is "Fire and Police Protection in the 1800s."

1. _____

2. _____

3. _____

4. _____

5. _____

© Houghton Mifflin Harcourt Publishing Company

Name _____ Date _____

E Read the ads below. Put a ✔ beside each ad that gives you the information you need to know about a product.

_____ 1.

> "Nothing can part me from my Tordack jeans!" says
> Sheila Jones, a top fashion model at the age of 13. Sheila's
> beauty has made her the one to watch for new fashion ideas.
> In her eighth-grade classes, you can always pick out Sheila.
> She's the one in the Tordack jeans!

_____ 2.

> **Special! Two days only! The popular Aardvark shirts are now only $10
> each. Made of fine cotton, these shirts are guaranteed, washable, and
> preshrunk. All sizes are available. Choose from frosty white, sunshine
> yellow, sky blue, emerald green, and shell pink.**

F Mrs. Wong, who is an author, was in Thailand to study the everyday life of the Thai people. Here are some articles she has written. Read the titles. Write *fact* next to the ones that *most likely* contain factual material. Write *fiction* next to the ones *most likely* to contain imaginary material.

1. Living Near Thailand's Canals _____

2. All About Thai Giants and Ogres _____

3. Animals of Thailand _____

4. How Elephants Are Trained _____

5. The Autobiography of the Thunder God _____

6. The Silkworm Speaks _____

7. Favorite Foods of the Thai People _____

8. The Climate of Thailand _____

9. How Thai Silk Is Made _____

10. Favorite Thai Myths _____

© Houghton Mifflin Harcourt Publishing Company

Answer Key

Selection 1: Paired
pages 1–5

A
1. b
2. c
3. a
4. d
5. c
6. a
7. d

B
1. The word *whop* imitates the sound of the steam-powered drill striking the steel spikes.
2. He was confident—maybe to the point of being prideful. The line "But before I let your steam drill beat me down / I'd die with a hammer in my hand" supports this.
3. John Henry won the contest because he managed to advance fifteen feet with the steel spikes, to the steam drill's nine feet. Yet, in another sense, John Henry lost the contest because winning it caused him to die.

C Dialect is used when someone is speaking; standard speech is used for the narration. The use of dialect helps the characters seem real, as well as to appear to be from another time in history.

D
1. John Henry was really a man who lived in the 1800s and worked laying down railroad tracks.
2. Yes. The introduction says that over the years different versions of the legend have been written, as well as songs based on the legend.
3. John Henry was heroic in his own way. But I can't tell how well known he was or whether his contest with the steam drill was famous.
4. "John Henry" was probably meaningful for other men who did the dangerous work of building railroad tracks.
5. Yes

Selection 2: Paired
pages 6–12

A
1. d
2. b
3. a
4. b
5. d
6. b
7. c
8. b

B
1. Bill had no problem living with coyotes for nine years; Bill was attracted to a stallion that no cowboy had been able to catch; Bill could talk to the stallion in the language of animals.
2. The author seems to admire Pecos Bill because of the way he or she described Bill's heroic adventure with Lightning in great detail. The author also seems to find Bill entertaining and enjoyable to write about. I think this because

the author includes many funny parts, such as the "yak, yak, yak" sound made by people who talked too much, according to Bill.

C
1. b; underline: knee-high to a grasshopper
2. a; underline: pulling my leg
3. g; underline: in hot pursuit
4. X
5. f; underline: Keep your chin up
6. e; underline: once in a blue moon
7. d; underline: tight-fisted
8. c; underline: a piece of cake

D
1. They both were very strong. They both made a great effort to reach a goal they had set for themselves.
2. I would consider only Pecos Bill completely successful because he was able to tame Lightning but did not get hurt or killed from doing it. John Henry was successful beating the steam drill, but he died right after that and was not able to enjoy his success.
3. The conflict is different. Pecos Bill was in conflict with a stallion, which is a part of nature. John Henry was in conflict with a machine, which is something produced by society.
4. Answers will vary. Possible answer: "John Henry": sorrowful, respectful, serious, sympathetic; "Pecos Bill": playful, humorous, admiring

E
1. a, c
2. a, b, d, f, g
3. Answers will vary.

Selection 3
pages 13–20

A
1. b
2. a
3. b
4. c
5. c
6. b

B
1. The author traces the history of the exchange of goods and services. Bartering took place before objects such as pieces of metal started to be used.
2. The paragraphs before it discuss bartering; the paragraphs after it discuss the development of coins.

C
1. divisible
2. designs
3. common
4. convenient
5. characteristic
6. garment
7. brilliant
8. swap
9. portable
10. durable
11. tampered

117

D 1. 6
2. *A History of Money in the American Colonies*
3. b
4. 2
5. Musket balls and nails were made in the colonies and traded.
6. d
7. a   9. d
8. 2   10. c

E 1. Spanish dollars
2. French ecus/Spanish bits
3. Dutch guilders
4. 11%
5. 8%
6. Spanish dollars/Dutch guilders
7. c
8. Foreign Coins Being Used in the United States in 1800

Selection 4
pages 21–28

A 1. b   5. c
2. b   6. a
3. c   7. b
4. d   8. b

B 1. The notes keep the story going forward, since the characters do things that the notes tell them to do.
2. A girl and her brother help their grandmother solve a mystery. The mystery is a search for a treasure that the deceased friend of their grandmother's left their grandmother. They find clues to where the treasure is located in rhymes hidden in pieces of furniture.

C 1. b   4. a
2. c   5. b
3. a   6. c

D 1. kill   6. water
2. dangerous   7. thermometer
3. snake   8. bee
4. nest   9. oven
5. summer

Selection 5
pages 29–39

A 1. a. an art teacher in school
   b. a neighbor who collects oil paintings
   c. the head librarian of the art library
   d. the director of the city museum

2. a. the director of the city museum
   b. the head librarian of the art library
   c. a neighbor who collects oil paintings
   d. an art teacher in school

B Answers will vary.

C 1. *European Art and Artists*
2. *A Guide to European Painters*
3. *Famous Artists and Their Works*
4. *Great Names in Art from the Fourteenth Century to the Seventeenth Century*
5. *Great Masterpieces of Belgium*

D 1. 307–637
2. 40–83; 85–98
3. 1300–1700
4. 495–520; 720–814; 819
5. b

E 1. jade   12. object
2. budge   13. search
3. trek   14. concealed
4. exclaim   15. obvious
5. hideous   16. shriek
6. wearily   17. ivory
7. persevere   18. grumble
8. tentacle   19. oriental
9. acquire   20. tiresome
10. suspense   21. priceless
11. antique

Dutch artist Jan Vermeer

Selection 6: Paired
pages 40–46

A 1. b   7. d
2. b   8. c
3. c   9. b
4. a   10. d
5. d   11. a
6. c

B 1. After he had escaped to New York, he changed his last name so it would be harder for the men pursuing him to find him.
2. This theme is brought up in the very first paragraph: Even as a young boy, Douglass knew he had to learn to read and write because he had realized that being educated was the only way he could become a free man.
3. The main text is mostly a series of facts about Douglass's life. Since these features contain Douglass's own words, they help to make him come alive for the reader.

© Houghton Mifflin Harcourt Publishing Company

Answer Key

Core Skills Reading Comprehension, Grade 6

C **1.** d **6.** h
2. i **7.** b
3. j **8.** g
4. a **9.** c
5. e **10.** f

Selection 7: Paired
pages 47–53

A **1.** a **4.** c
2. c **5.** d
3. b **6.** a

B **1.** It was an exchange. He gave them bread and, in return, they give him reading lessons.
2. As a boy, Frederick Douglass was determined to learn to read and write. He would ask poor boys in his neighborhood to give him a reading lesson in exchange for bread. The boys would express their sympathy when he reminded them that he would always be a slave.

C **1.** convert **7.** compelled
2. prudence **8.** unpardonable
3. console **9.** tempted
4. bestow **10.** offense
5. accomplish **11.** testimonial
6. urchin **12.** gratitude

D **1.** Bread gives your body nourishment. Since Douglass believed that knowledge would eventually help him escape slavery, knowledge was a kind of emotional nourishment that helped him stand being a slave.
2. Meat can represent all food. Having something to eat and drink is necessary to live. For Douglass, at that time in his life the newspaper was so important to him that it seemed almost a necessity.
3–7. Answers will vary.

E **1.** Since it was an "unpardonable offence" to teach slaves to read, few people were willing to do it. Douglass's second master's wife taught him basic reading until her husband commanded her to stop. A free black man taught him to read the Bible. He got neighborhood boys to give him lessons in exchange for bread. But none of these people were "regular" teachers.
2. The boys were willing to help Douglass learn how to read. The two masters would not allow any slave to learn to read. The boys had sympathy for him that he would be a slave his entire life. The two masters probably did not have any sympathy that he would always be a slave.
3a. The poor boys in his neighborhood helped him with reading lessons.

3b. Sofia Auld, the wife of Douglass's second master, was teaching him to read until her husband commanded her to stop. Douglass learned to read the Bible in Dr. Lewis G. Wells's Bible classes.
4. The author of "Frederick Douglass: Abolitionist Leader" told the events of Frederick Douglass's life in chronological order, beginning with his childhood and ending with his death. The autobiography excerpt is mainly the presentation of a main idea—Douglass's desire to learn to read—and details about his plan that helped him achieve this.
5. Frederick Douglass wrote about his life probably to share with readers how terrible it was to be a slave and how much determination it took to become a free man. The author of "Frederick Douglass: Abolitionist Leader" probably wrote the selection for two reasons: to give facts about Douglass's life and to provide reasons why he should be admired.
6. For the most part, the tone of "Frederick Douglass: Abolitionist Leader" is informative. Except for the "A Voice from the Past" features, the selection is a set of facts about events in Douglass's life. Yet there is also a tone of admiration. The tone of Douglass's autobiography is reflective. He is thinking back to an early time in his life. The tone is also solemn because the events he describes are very serious.
7. Answers will vary.

Skills Review: Selections 1–7
pages 54–60

A Check ✓1., 2., 5., and 6.

B **1.** e; underline: beating around the bush
2. b: underline: backward and forward
3. d; underline: bent out of shape
4. c; underline: get a kick out of
5. a; underline: had his hands full

C **1.** drive **4.** desert
2. fish **5.** aunt
3. scent

D **1.** c **5.** c
2. a **6.** a
3. a **7.** b
4. b **8.** c

E **1.** a.
2. d. or g.
3. c
4. f
5. e. or g.

© Houghton Mifflin Harcourt Publishing Company

F 1. 187–189, 193–197, 200
  2. 4
  3. no
  4. 16, 20–21
  5. Origin
  6. 167, 171
  7. early Europe
  8. 125 or 198
  9. 150–159
  10. Eskimos
  11. Origin
  12. 16, 20–21

G I. A. 1. Philodendrons
  I. A. 4. Poinsettias
  I. B. Leaves poisonous if eaten
  II. Poisonous wild plants
  II. A. Poison ivy and poison sumac
  II. A. 3. Cause blisters, red skin, and itching
  II. B. The datura plant
  II. B. 2. All parts poisonous if touched
  II. B. 4. Causes nervous twitching
  II. B. 6. Large quantity causes unconsciousness and death
  II. C. Wild mushrooms
  II. C. 2. Harmless and harmful mushrooms look alike

Selection 8
pages 61–68

A 1. c   3. d
  2. d   4. b

B 2. flowers—pale yellow
  3. tug-of-war—monkey and blossom
  4. Ethan squash—hairy spider
  5. crocodile—Jaime

C 1. equator
  2. South America
  3. United States
  4. North America
  5. southeast

D 1. hotter   5. very cold
  2. cooler   6. near
  3. colder   7. hot, high
  4. warmer   8. northwest

E 1. false   7. false
  2. true   8. false
  3. false   9. true
  4. false   10. false
  5. true   11. true
  6. false   12. true

F 1. temperature 9. comb
  2. scramble 10. attract
  3. screech 11. burro
  4. observed 12. jungle
  5. humidity 13. squash
  6. journey 14. routine
  7. failure 15. strength
  8. vine 16. fragrance

Selection 9
pages 69–75

A 1. a   4. a
  2. d   5. c
  3. c

B 1. The girls turned pale, showing that they were scared and worried. This was a natural reaction to a dangerous situation. But because "their jungle training had taught them to think quickly," they immediately went into action—Rosa to help Ethan stay calm and Amanda to go get help from the adults.
  2. At first, the kids were enjoying their search for unusual birds in the rain forest. Then they encountered some of the dangers of the rain forest—a boa and a deep pit—and were put in danger.
  3. While the kids were bird watching, they met with danger. A boa wrapped itself around Ethan, and Jaime fell into a pit and disappeared. Rosa stayed with Ethan to help him stay calm, and Amanda went for help. Ethan was safe after the boa slithered away, but the adults could not locate Jaime.

C 1. a. Main Idea
  b. Detail
  c. Detail
  d. Detail
  e. Detail
  f. Detail
  2. a. Detail
  b. Detail
  c. Detail
  d. Main Idea
  e. Detail

D 1. b   4. c
  2. a   5. c
  3. c

© Houghton Mifflin Harcourt Publishing Company

E **1.** What a struggle it was just to walk through the rain forest.
2. Tarantulas—very large, hairy spiders—are dangerous to man and beast.
3. To be a fish, a creature must have fins, gills, and a backbone.
4. In general, animals choose the location of their nests and homes carefully.

Selection 10
pages 76–84

A **1.** c **4.** b
2. c **5.** d
3. a **6.** b

B **1.** to mention the other characters one more time before the story ended; to create suspense
2. The scientists finally located the Mysterias only after Jaime accidentally fell into the pit, was carried down the river, squeezed through the crevice in the cave wall, and saw them in the meadow outside the cave.

C Order may vary.
1. fragrance **2.** scent
3. sniff **4.** breathe
5. odor **6.** aroma
7. inhale **8.** stink

D **1.** The swimmers were *plunging* into the river.
2. The current of the river moved *swiftly.*
3. Jaime *carefully* broke the stem of the flower.
4. He was *tossed* like a bouncing ball.
5. The bloodhound *tracked* the lost camper.

E **1.** Underline: Insects live in almost every kind of place.
Draw a line through these sentences:
Insects fly, crawl, hop, jump, walk, and swim.
Insects can be different sizes and different colors.
2. Underline: All insects have these things in common.
Draw a line through this sentence:
There are more insects in the world than all other animals put together.

F **1.** Kinds of Waterfalls
2. The Formation of Waterfalls
3. A Useful Animal
4. A Stubborn Animal

G **1.** e **4.** c
2. d **5.** a
3. b **6.** b

H **1.** The heads of moths and butterflies, like the heads of humans, have important uses.
2. d
3. c
4. c
5. 1. e
2. c
3. a
4. d
5. b
6. d

Selection 11
pages 85–92

A **1.** b **4.** b
2. d **5.** c
3. a

B **1.** At first the tone is pleasant and practical. It changes when the creature's flipper pushes back the vine leaves and its face appears above the nest. The author's use of *gigantic, roughly, tremendous,* and *threatening* help to change the tone.
2. For Jaime the rain forest means his only chance of being rescued. That is why he spends time there.
3. a. boy; b. shorts; c. hand; d. hair

C **1.** 30
2. August
3. 11
4. 1 week, 4 days
5. 21
6. October 1
7. September 14
8. September

D **1.** toting
2. neglect
3. apologize
4. clammy
5. gleaming
6. conceal
7. intervene
8. talons
9. dense
10. quiver
11. haste

© Houghton Mifflin Harcourt Publishing Company

Selection 12
pages 93–99

A 1. c   4. b
   2. d   5. c
   3. b

B 1. Maykala was fun-loving and made many friends. Her nature was to enjoy herself. Ramasoon was always angry and did things that could hurt the humans living on the earth.
   2. lightning: Maykala made the sun reflect off her crystal ball to momentarily blind Ramasoon; thunder: Ramasoon threw his ax at Maykala, but it fell to the earth when the ax missed her; heavy rain: Ramasoon freed the dark rain clouds that his cape held

C 1. recall, forget
   2. glaring, smiling
   3. gigantic, tiny
   4. serious, fun-loving
   5. catch, pursue
   6. scatter, collect
   7. momentarily, permanently

D 1. what happened when winter came
   2. how sunshine on the waves made them glitter
   3. how day and night came about

E 1. d   6. b
   2. g   7. e
   3. j   8. f, h
   4. i   9. h
   5. a   10. c

Selection 13
pages 100–112

A 1. fiction   3. fact
   2. fact   4. fact

B 1. d   4. b
   2. b   5. a
   3. c   6. c

C 1. with a description of his superstition about photographing a skydiver on Friday the thirteenth
   2. It helps me understand what is was like for Adam North to have the parachute wrapped around his body like a plastic bag—and, since he was falling headfirst, also to understand how dangerous his situation was.

D 1. ✓   4. 3
   2. 1   5. 2
   3. ✓

E 1. survivors   4. bear
   2. superstitious   5. gear
   3. gear   6. reserve

F Circle 2, 5, 7, 8.

G 1. fact   5. fact
   2. fact   6. fiction
   3. fiction   7. fact
   4. fiction

H 2. relevant
   3. relevant
   4. Underline: *A book entitled United States History from 1850 to 1980* was published in 1982.
   5. relevant
   6. Underline: In the November issue are these three stories: "A Schoolboy of Old Wyoming"; "Beulah, a Girl of Colonial Georgia"; and "Fiona and Angus of Virginia."
   7. relevant

Skills Review: Selections 8–13
pages 113–116

A 1. trembling, still
   2. heal, injure
   3. survivor, victim
   4. grab, release

B 1. sturdy, stable
   2. convince, persuade
   3. rotate, spin
   4. glittering, dazzling

C Underline:
   1. If a sunflower is in a garden with many other kinds of flowers, it will be the first one noticed.
   2. The sunflower head, which is shaped like a very large daisy, is colorful.
   3. Sunflowers always face the light.
   4. It is clear that sunflower seeds are very useful.

   1. c
   2. how sunflowers move
   3. Paragraph 4
   4. a

D Picture 1: e, g, i, l
   Picture 2: a, c, f, h, k

E Check ✓2.

F 1. fact   6. fiction
   2. fiction   7. fact
   3. fact   8. fact
   4. fact   9. fact
   5. fiction   10. fiction

122